total!
PSION
beginners

Mark Webb

Bruce Smith Books

Total! PSION beginners

© Mark Webb
ISBN: 1-873308-26-4
First Edition: March 1997

Editor: Anne Bartasiene
Typesetting: Bruce Smith Books Ltd
Series Cover Design: Bruce Smith

Published by:
Bruce Smith Books, PO Box 382, St Albans, Herts, AL2 3BR
email: Mark-Webb@msn.com

Printed – on paper from chlorine-free pulp from managed forests – and bound in the UK by Ashford Colour Press

The Author

Mark Webb is, first and foremost, an avid user of his Psion Series 3. He is a full-time editor of computer publications at Bruce Smith Books. A former group editor of *A&B Computing*, *Electronics Today International* and other specialist computer magazines, he is also the author of the *PC Multimedia Insider Guide* and *Mastering Amiga for Beginners*.

Mark's other interests include watching football, rugby and cricket plus cycling and real ale – and often combinations of all of these.

Contents

What's in this Book for You?

The aim of this book is to help you get the best from your Psion palmtop computer. You will learn how to use the Psion Series 3 range of palmtop computers through menus and keypresses, how to work with files and how to fully exploit the extensive built-in software for your everyday use.

The Psion Series 3 range of portable, *indeed* pocket-sized, computers comprises the Series 3c, Siena, Series 3a and Workabout models. This book is also applicable to the Acorn Pocket Book II because this palmtop, which is widely used in schools, is entirely based on the Psion Series 3a. A special chapter is provided to cover its particular characteristics and uses.

The Psion range is a remarkable success story in many ways. To name just two: commercial success and wide acceptance to rival the big world brands of portable computing; and a unique technology and design which is appealing, practical and full of possibilities.

It's this last point which I hope to explore together with you in this book. It's a book suitable for beginners to computing with the Psion Series 3 and compatibles. If you've had some experience of desktop computers then you'll find some aspects of the Psion Series 3 familiar, other aspects less obvious, others entirely new.

You'll find the early chapters easy to follow, with plenty of examples to try out. Later chapters delve deeper into the software and investigate more ambitious projects. In addition you'll find out how to use your Psion with a PC by using PsiWin, and how to send faxes and electronic mail (email). There are handy references to *hot-key* presses, *menus,* the *filing system*, *add-ons*, public domain software, *on-line* services, clubs, publications and more. If it's anything to do with using your Psion you should find it here. This book is not a guide to programming your Psion. It *is* about effective use of the many features and functions – productivity tools if you like – which you'll find in your Psion.

Planning Ahead

Using the Psion Series 3 is fun but we're all in the productivity game, trying to grab some leisure time by getting our work done efficiently. To this end, we'll work through the *time management* features of the Psion Series 3 and push the *wordprocessing, spreadsheet* and *database* into some interesting areas. There's a lot to discover and to put to work on your behalf.

As with any computer software designed by human ingenuity, the Psion Series 3 software has its quirks and its shortcuts. Because of the number and depth of features in some *applications,* it's necessary to plan the use of the software before proceeding. In all these matters, this book will help you find the best routes to success as quickly as possible. By the way 'application' is what Psion call a 'computer program'. I've tried to use Psion's own terms, especially those used on screen, in this book.

Those of you who use a desktop PC will probably know that the Psion Series 3 can be connected to a desktop computer and information transferred between them. In this book we'll go step by step through this process to show how it can best be done.

An associated topic, and a hot topic in personal computing, is electronic mail and on-line information services, the Internet and the associated hype. We'll establish communications with the Psion Series 3 to exploit some of these new possibilites.

Models

The company Psion, as opposed to the computer, has been around since the start of personal computing in the UK and the Organiser, which came before the Series 3 and 3a, blazed the trail for hand-held computing. Marks & Spencer famously used the Organiser to keep track of stock on its shelves and the Organiser found acceptance in the commercial world at a time when today's luggable computers were called 'portable'.

The Psion Series 3 came next and broadened the overall appeal of the palm-top computer. The Psion Series 3a succeeded it, bringing a screen twice the size, some new versions of built-in software, and in the 1Mb and 2Mb models extra built-in software in the form of the Speller and Thesaurus applications plus a Patience game.

Most recently Psion launched the Series 3c and Siena. Once again the built-in software was enhanced. If you own a Series 3c or Siena then you'll find extra sections in parts of this book to cover extra features in the software you are using. For instance your Psion Series 3c or Siena contains two modes of using the Calc application, both of which are covered in its own chapter.

The main difference between the various Series 3 models is the amount of memory in each. As each model has appeared with more available memory the 'memory for your money' equation has improved for the purchaser. In the meantime existing owners of Series 3 computers have been able to upgrade their memory, and applications, to suit.

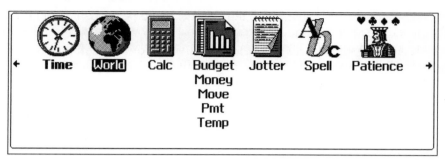

The Psion Series 3c and Siena are the latest Psion models and additional software features are covered in each chapter in this book, as appropriate.

Everything in this book relates to all Psion Series 3a palmtops except the following:

• Spelling and Thesaurus applications, which are not available on the Series 3a models with smaller memory sizes (e.g. 512K and below).

• additional software features introduced in the Series 3c (e.g. Jotter application).

Most of this book is also applicable to the earlier Psion Series 3 model (Acorn Pocket Book I) with only the Agenda application having changed out of recognition.

Everything in this book is also relevant to users of the the Acorn Pocket Book II. The Pocket Book is an Acorn-badged version of the Series 3a with additional software and peripherals to make it suitable for use in schools, alongside other Acorn desktop computers.

Conventions

There are few complications in describing the operation of the Psion Series 3. Menu options are referred to by the names which appear in the Psion Series 3 drop-down menus and the equivalent keyboard shortcut (see below) is also given. Text displayed on screen is printed as it appears.

I have put menu items and other messages displayed on the screen between single quotes, e.g. 'Set alarm' and 'Esc to continue' where it's necessary to make it clear what is being talked about. I've used a simple convention to show the menu tree structure. For instance I refer to the Insert text function in the Edit menu as Edit/Insert text. The / key indicates a second level of menu and there are rarely more than two levels of menu in Psion Series 3 applications.

Messages are always displayed as they appear. In some cases I've laid out a display the way it looks on screen and the text is shown in a slightly different style to indicate that you should view this as the equivalent of the text which appears on the Psion Series 3 screen, for example:

Name: Brian Smith

Work: 01234 567891

Address:

Notes:

which shows a possible record card in the Database application. You'll also see illustrations from the Psion's screen. These pictures have been captured directly from the screen. I've put the most important activities which you will carry out on your Psion into something I've named the *PsiGuide*. The PsiGuide is a sequence of screen pictures with a text commentary. Follow a PsiGuide the first time to discover how to carry out a task. Later, if you forget how to do something, look up the subject in the index and you'll find there's a PsiGuide to take you through it again.

The Psion Series 3 keyboard. It's a familiar QWERTY layout with the 'computer' keys such as Control and Esc. The Menu, Psion (∪) and ♦ keys are grouped in the bottom left-hand corner.

Special Keys

There are two ways to turn on the Psion Series 3, one is to use the ON key (Esc), the other is to press one of the pictures on the front panel, below the screen. Although these *icons* are shown in the book, I don't use them to denote the applications they represent, e.g. I simply write 'press the Sheet icon'.

The Psion Series 3 has a pretty standard computer keyboard and, when referring to a key, I use the spelling of the key on the keyboard and screen. An example is 'press Tab'. If it's not clear that a keyboard key is intended then I've put the key in between single quotes, for example press the '1' key.

There are a few special keys which are used alone or in conjunction with the number and letter keys to perform certain tasks. All will become clear in the chapters to come but it's worth mentioning now that I've picked out these keys in the text through the use of special characters.

The Psion key is the left-most key on the bottom row. It has an unusual character on it which I've reproduced in the text as ∪. The keys which have yellow text above them have special purposes or produce different characters when pressed in conjunction with the Psion key.

An example of a special function is when you press the Psion (∪) key and the < key, it adjusts the contrast of the screen display. An example of a special character is when you press the Psion key and the 6 key in combination, the character produced is @.

Two important keys with yellow text above them are Esc and 1. Esc also acts as the ON key but this is the one exception because you don't need to press the Psion key as well. When you press ∪1 it turns the Psion Series 3 OFF.

Two further keys which work in conjunction with others are the Shift and Control keys. Shift works with alphabetic characters to upper case (i.e. capital letters) and also together with the Psion key to instigate menu functions. For instance pressing Shift, ∪ and X (Shift∪X) in combination leaves an application and doesn't save any changes you've made. The Control key is used in conjunction with the arrow keys and this combination is simply explained in the text as 'Control key and up arrow key' or similar.

Another unfamiliar key is ♦. The ♦ key is used to move between different *modes* of operation inside applications, more of which in the relevant chapters. When you press the ∪♦ keys in combination, it acts as a 'caps lock' key which forces all alphabetic characters you type to appear in upper case. Press ∪♦ again to turn the caps lock off and return to normal lower case letters.

The keys with arrows on them grouped in the bottom right-hand corner of the keyboard, are used to move around the screen. Obviously enough, I call them the 'arrow keys'. The Menu key is referred to simply as Menu e.g. 'press Menu'.

Pocketable

These ground rules will be useful to you as you read the rest of the book. In producing the book, I've tried to balance the fact that there's a lot of information to pack in against the knowledge that the book will inevitably be less portable than the computer I'm writing about! C'est la vie!

Chapter 1

What is the Psion Palmtop?

What is the Psion Series 3? What is the Psion Series 3 palmtop? What makes it tick and how can you use it in your everyday work and play? This is where the adventure begins.

What is the Psion Series 3?

You may not have asked yourself this question even when you were weighing up the purchase of a portable computer. I'm not going to discuss the Psion Series 3 in relation to any of its portable, laptop or handheld rivals but it's worth asking what the Psion Series 3 is made of, so to speak.

Naturally it's silicon chips and tracks and cable and plastic. It's definitely hardware – small and robust. It's definitely software – icons and words appear on the screen when you press the ON key. It's definitely a personal computer with keyboard, screen and port to the world outside. It's not a big calculator, rather a small personal computer.

The Psion Series 3 is different from any other computer I know so, even if you've owned a computer before, keep reading to get some background on how the Psion Series 3 does what it does. It will help when you get into the in-built software later because the way the computer applications in the Psion Series 3 work is closely related to the nature of the Psion Series 3 palmtop itself.

Winning Recipe

The Psion Series 3 is a great piece of design, a 6 inch x 3 inch x 1 inch computer. It's hi-tech in a '30s cigarette case sort of way. Have you seen the wood finish version? Wow! or Wow? There's a way into the apparently seamless shell but it's not immediately obvious. If you half open the Psion Series 3 it reveals itself to be two separate units connected by a ribbon cable.

The Psion Series 3 is, like other computers, a combination of physical components (hardware) and invisible instructions (software). The hardware encompasses everything from the brilliantly designed case, the Liquid Crystal Display (LCD) screen, the keyboard, the circuit board inside which provides the complex connections between the chips, and the chips themselves.

These are silicon chips of various kinds, often with a specific job to do, for instance to generate the screen display. The all-purpose chip is the central processing unit (CPU) or 'processor' for short. This chip processes software instructions and all the applications you use in the Psion Series 3 operate by sending instructions to the CPU. There are millions of instructions in a constant stream, monitoring the keyboard to see if you've pressed it, checking the cursor position to look up the right menu to put on your screen or changing a piece of information in the computer's memory.

The applications – lists of instructions – which appear on the System screen when you first turn on your Psion Series 3 are permanently stored inside chips in the Psion Series 3. The chips are Read Only Memory (ROM), computer memory from which information can flow but which can't be changed in any way.

Memories

Read Only Memory (ROM) is one of three kinds of memory which you can use in your Psion Series 3. The second type is Random Access Memory (RAM), which is where you store information created on your Psion Series 3. The shopping list you type into Word is in the RAM of the Psion Series 3, either in an open Word *document* or as a *file* saved from Word, or both.

The reason you don't lose that shopping list when you turn off your Psion Series 3 is that the RAM is 'battery-backed'. In other words, the batteries in your Psion Series 3 supply electrical current to the RAM which keeps the information stored there 'fresh'. In fact it's probably better to think in terms of putting your Psion Series 3 into a 'resting' state or as 'powered down' or 'in suspended animation', rather than 'turned off'. It's only really turned off when both sets of batteries – main and backup – fail completely and this is only likely to happen if you put your Psion Series 3 away for a very long time indeed and forget about it.

The third kind of memory doesn't come as a standard item but is an upgrade item for your Psion Series 3 – see the appropriate appendix. If you flip your Psion Series 3 over, right to left, and look at the bottom you'll see the speaker in the middle and on the left and right there are two hinged 'doors' which are marked B (left) and A (right). The left-hand slot beneath the door contains a lithium battery – 3v 1620– which is the backup battery, the last resort to keep the data held in the Psion Series 3's RAM intact!

The compartment below door A is empty but, and this is where we get interested, it's ready to hold a solid state disk (SSD). This is the third type of RAM and it's the latest thing in computer memory storage devices and ideal for computing on the move.

Solid State Disks extend the memory of your Psion.

Even the SSDs come in two forms. The first is the equivalent of ROM. When you insert the SSD the System screen is updated to show you the contents of the disk. The contents can be accessed but you can't save data to this type of SSD, only to your internal disk. The second form of SSD is called 'flash' SSD and this refers to 'flash' memory, a type of memory which can be 'changed' to store data in a manner similar to changing a magnetic medium such as floppy or hard disk. A flash SSD is not only empty when you get it, it is also 'blank', known as 'unformatted'.

Before the Psion Series 3's filing system can store data on a flash SSD, it needs to put down some electronic signposts and addresses on the 'blank' disk. It does this during the formatting process and, once complete, the storage on the flash SSD is available to Psion Series 3 applications in the same manner as the internal disk. There is however an underlying difference which you should be aware of. Saving information onto a flash SSD uses up more battery power than saving onto the internal disk.

There is a mains power supply unit (PSU) available for the Psion Series 3 – see the appendix on add-ons – and this may prove a good buy if you're going to purchase, format and use a lot of flash SSDs. As far as we're concerned, a SSD is another way of adding storage to the Psion Series 3. The SSD is configured as a disk and it appears as a disk to the applications you use. So too does some of the internal RAM of the Psion Series 3, configured as the 'internal disk'.

Disks and Files

To some extent it doesn't matter which type of memory is in the Psion Series 3, rather how it is presented to us through the Psion Series 3's disk operating/filing system. If you want an analogy from the world of desktop computers then you are using the same memory for applications and data and also for a RAM disk. You can configure RAM disks on DOS, Acorn, Mac and Amiga computers. They are 'made' out of memory but act like floppy disks. They are usually impermanent on desktop computers whereas on the Psion Series 3 the internal disk is battery-backed, like the rest of the memory.

The Psion Series 3's disk operating system (DOS) is effectively put to work from the System screen which is the focal point of using the Psion Series 3, and which I'll introduce in the next chapter. The use of applications from the System screen is mixed in with the operation of disk filing commands which work on files in a part of the memory of the Psion Series 3. The Psion Series 3's memory is organised into blocks and some of it has been given the properties which are associated with physical disks – floppy and hard – on desktop computers.

If floppies and hard drives are familiar devices to you then all the better because this familiarity will help you control your Psion Series 3. If they are not familiar then it remains of interest that the internal disk drive of the Psion Series 3 is very similar to that of a standard personal computer – the type that is referred to as 'IBM compatible' or 'runs DOS' or 'runs Windows' or 'runs Windows 95'.

The types of storage you don't have on your Psion Series 3, but which you might have encountered on a desktop computer, are floppy disk and hard disk. The Psion Series 3 has room for neither, and you don't need them. Adding standard PC type peripherals to a Psion Series 3 is not an option.

Psion keyboards (Siena above) are tiny and you'll need to develop a technique for entering information quickly and correctly.

Hands On

So, we've covered the processing and the storage. How do we use them? Simply, through the keyboard and screen. The keyboard – layout and keys – is discussed in detail later but it's worth noting a few facts of life at this stage. The keys are very small. This makes the Psion Series 3 a great computer for young children, but you can't touch type with an adult hand. You'll need to develop your own technique.

I'm usually holding the Psion Series 3 with one hand so I practise using the other hand to type and, depending on how dextrous you are, you can evolve a form of touch-typing with one hand. In other words, using all the fingers of the one hand to cover the keyboard rather than picking out each key in turn with the index finger.

If, however, you are a quick 'two-fingered' typist then you'll probably get on well by adapting your technique to the smaller size, one or two-handed. It's certainly worth trying to keep the key presses to a minimum and to this end you should practice the key short-cuts which are given throughout this book. If you do so, you'll find them coming naturally to mind after a while.

There are also some efficient routes you can take when navigating the menus and you'll discover these as we roam though the applications in later chapters. You can get a lot out of the Psion Series 3 when you know how.

When you press the keyboard the Psion Series 3 takes notice and responds with an action of some kind, the result of which you can see on the screen. Pressing an arrow key results in the cursor or highlight moving position. Pressing the ◆ key results in a new display and so on.

You can set different zoom sizes to use the Psion screen to best effect.

In View

The screen is a LCD (Liquid Crystal Display) unit which gives you a view of what's 'in' the Psion Series 3. When a document, such as a letter or spreadsheet, is bigger than the screen can display, the arrow key can be used to move around the whole document and to bring into view the part you wish to work on.

The LCD screen is the sort used on cameras and camcorders. It can only display black and white and it needs some form of external light for you to be able to see it – it doesn't glow in the dark! The grey shades you can see on the icons on screen are created by mixing tightly-packed black and white pixels. Pixels (picture elements) are electronic 'dots' which are turned either on or off for black or white.

The Psion Series 3's operating system builds the picture from these building blocks and fixed combinations of pixels which form characters, such as A to Z, 0 to 9 and other characters such as blocks and lines.

Lend an Ear

That nearly completes our short tour of the Psion Series 3, the bits they call 'hardware'. There's one last interesting feature of the Psion Series 3 which needs noting and that's its sound capability. Two components enable the Psion Series 3 to make a sound and record a sound.

The loudspeaker is located on the bottom of the unit and generates a sound you can hear some few feet away. It also contains a magnet which can wipe the magnetic strip on your credit card – as I found to my annoyance! Psion's manual contains a clear warning but too late! The Psion Series 3 tucks so snugly into my jacket pocket. Now till assistants at stations and supermarkets frown as nothing happens after their 'swipe' and I explain they'll just have to type in the number. Just warning you!

The microphone enables the Psion Series 3 to record a sound. It's so tiny you could easily miss it on the right-hand bottom edge just in front of the 'B' slot. You can speak into this microphone to record messages and alarms, both of which can be very useful.

OS

Running all this equipment packed into a palm-sized computer is an operating system (OS). It's what makes the whole thing tick and we'll try it out in the next chapter.

Psion make their 16-bit Epoc operating system available to third parties so we may find Series 3a look-alikes appearing from other companies to bolster the ranks of Psion fans. There's also an Epoc/32 operating system being developed for future Psion products so there's an exciting future ahead for palmtop users.

Chapter 2

Getting Started: Push for Go

Pressing buttons and filling in forms is how you operate your Psion Series 3. Starting to use your Psion Series 3 is as easy as pushing a button. Sit your Psion Series 3 down with Psion logo on top, pull the screen up and back on its hinge and press the ON button at the top left of the keyboard. If your Psion Series 3 hasn't been used recently then you'll activate the System screen.

Think of System as an application for organising your organiser! You can carry out all sorts of operations from here, including the selection of other applications, but you needn't visit here at all if you want to use one of the other applications.

To start any application in the Psion Series 3 you just press its icon on the front panel and it leaps out of its dormant state. The Psion Series 3 is 'dormant' not 'off' because the batteries are providing a tiny electrical current which allows the internal memory of the Psion Series 3 to retain the information you've entered into it. Plainly the Psion Series 3 is also keeping tabs on the icon strip below the screen, checking continuously to see if you've pressed one! It makes you tired just thinking about the long hours your Psion Series 3 spends waiting for your touch!

From the icon strip you can go into eight of the different applications which come with the Psion Series 3. There are more than eight applications in the Psion Series 3 but the main applications are represented by the icons on the front. You can assign a different application to one of these icons if you wish, more of which later. You'll encounter two different ways of activating an application so, since we are just starting out, let's see both in action.

Press On

Press the Time (clock) icon on the icon strip which nestles below the screen and you'll go straight into the clock application, displaying the current time and date on the right and a list of empty alarms on the left.

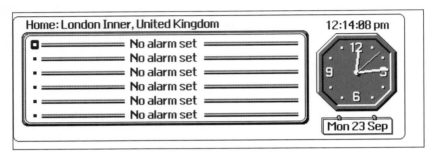

Time is the exception which proves the rule. There are no files associated with it, so pressing the icon takes you straight into the application. It's effectively 'active' all of the time.

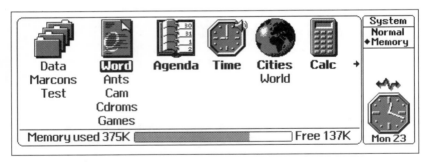

Now press on the Word icon and you'll find the System screen appear. It's not a mistake. Note that the first listed file name 'Word' is highlighted beneath the icon of the Word application displayed on screen. The application is not yet 'active' or 'open' and therefore your Psion Series 3 has put you into the System screen, at the ready with the only file available highlighted. In the picture *above* there is more than one file to choose from. When you first start your Psion Series 3, only Word is listed. After subsequent use, another file name may be highlighted first in the list.

To open a document called Word in the Word application, just press the Enter key. "Word opened" will display in the bottom right-hand corner and you are presented with a screen with a thin black line around it, an arrowhead to show you which line you are on and a flashing cursor. On the right-hand side is a separate box containing the document's name at the top, the words Normal and Outline and the clock still ticking away.

Hidden Activity

There's lots more to the Word application of course and we'll fully investigate it later. For now, press and hold down the Z key for a few seconds. Now press the Psion key and hold it down, and then press the 1 (OFF) key. The screen goes blank. Now press the Word icon and you'll find that the Word document appears immediately and you'll see the Zs which you typed, proving it's the same document.

Because Word was already active, your pressing the icon has taken you directly into the application and into the open document. In other words whenever the Psion is switched on, it will display the last 'active' screen, at the point it was switched off. You have now seen two of the different ways in which the Psion Series 3 responds to your key presses, depending on the state of the applications inside.

Turn off your Psion Series 3 again and this time press the Sheet icon. You'll get its picture (icon) on the System screen and its name below, highlighted in black. When I write 'highlighted' in this book I mean that the text is shown as white on a black background. This is the reverse of the normal black on a white background and is also known as 'inverse video'.

When a name is highlighted like this it means it is selected and pressing Enter activates the selected application. To select another application use the arrow keys and you'll see the highlight move to another application name. Using the arrow keys (also known as *cursor keys* because they move the cursor) is a basic way of choosing something else displayed on the Psion Series 3 screen.

Flexibility

One of the great things about the Psion Series 3 is its flexibility. Not in the 'flexible friend' sense but in the way that you can make it work to suit you. The options are not boundless of course but the designers have thought through some alternative ways of working which you can choose from.

Carrying out such 'housekeeping' activities is OK if you only have to do them occasionally, a fact which applies both in the house and with your Psion Series 3. So the key is to find out how you like things to work and to set them up that way once and for all.

The place to do this 'setting up' is the System screen so, if you are not already in the System screen, press the System icon to activate it ready to carry out some of the instructions below. The first change you may like to make is to the time it takes for the Psion Series 3 to switch itself off when there is no activity on the keyboard.

The Psion Series 3 is very economical with battery power; nevertheless prolonging battery life is worthwhile and the Psion Series 3 is using more power when it's on than when it's dormant. It makes sense therefore to adjust the time that the Psion Series 3 stays on when you are not using it and you do this by cutting down the time from the standard (default) setting of five minutes, which I think is a long time to not touch the keyboard.

To change the setting, go through the following sequence of key presses

> **Menu** *(a list of items associated with File will appear)*
>
> **Right arrow key four times onto Control** *(the first item Sound will be highlighted)*
>
> **Down arrow key twice down to Auto switch off**
>
> **Enter** *(see screen shot below)*
>
> **Down arrow key once to 'Switch off time'**
>
> **Right arrow key once and type '01'**
>
> **Enter**

If you agree that five minutes (default as in picture above) is a bit long then I suggest you bring it down to one minute by carrying out the instructions given above. After pressing Enter you will return to the System screen. The switch off time allows for hours, minutes and seconds so you've got plenty of scope. Anywhere between one minute and three minutes I find acceptable so I choose the lower limit to conserve batteries when I'm off day-dreaming. The switch off time is not timed from switching on the Psion Series 3 but from the last time you pressed the keyboard.

Hot-keys

Incidentally when you made the change above you used a menu and you used a dialogue box, two key features of operating your Psion Series 3, both of which are fully discussed in the next chapter. There is a way of getting to the destination dialogue box which is faster than the key sequence above and it's called 'using a hot-key'.

A hot-key is a key or combination of keys which, when pressed at the same time, call up a particular part of an application. In the case of the Auto switch off setting dialogue box, the hot-key combination is ∪O. Press the Psion key and, while still holding down the Psion key, press the O key. Up pops the dialogue you've just used.

There's more on hot-keys in the next chapter and you'll see that they are scattered about the book to remind you of the shortcuts which are available. Also there's an appendix which gives all the hot-keys for all the menus in your Psion Series 3 which you can use as a reference any time you need to look up a hot-key combination for a menu option or other function.

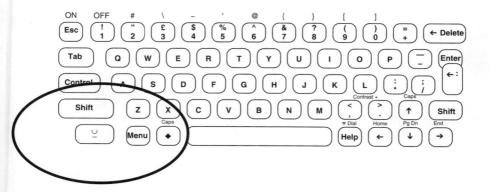

The Psion key and the Shift and Psion keys work in combination with other single keys to provide quick access to menu items and other functions.

System Views

You've now experienced how the System screen is a gateway to other applications which reside in the Psion Series 3 and is also a place to change settings in the Psion Series 3 i.e. the 'timeout' we adjusted previously. You'll have noticed that there is information about your Psion Series 3 displayed on the System screen. The main window contains the icons of the applications, not all of which fit into the display so you'll see an arrow on the right-hand side indicating that the display can be moved to view additional icons.

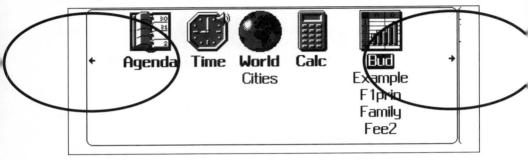

Press the right-facing arrow key to move the highlight to the right. The display 'scrolls' and you'll notice an arrow appear on the left-hand side of the window to indicate that you've left part of the display behind. Keep moving to the right until you see the OPL Program icon.

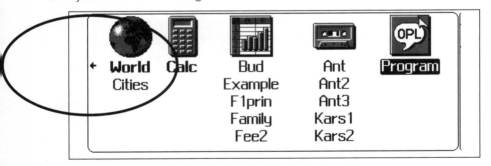

This is the right-hand edge of the display so the arrow on the right disappears to indicate that there is no more to display. Try pressing ∪ together with the left/right arrow keys to move from one end of the display to another.

The size of the display can be adjusted in any Psion Series 3 application and System is no exception. The Zoom, i.e. size-change, facility will be investigated further during the course of the book but for the moment give this hot-key press a try and leave the display at the size you prefer:

Hold down the Psion key and press the Z key (∪Z), wait to see the new view and, keeping the Psion key pressed, press the Z key again (∪Z). Keep pressing and you'll get around to the display you started with.

More Screen

If you don't want the clock display taking up space down the right-hand side of the screen then hold down the Control key and press the Menu key at the same time. Press the Menu key a few times to see the different possibilities. This is available in the System screen and in applications such as Word, where it usefully expands the area available for working in.

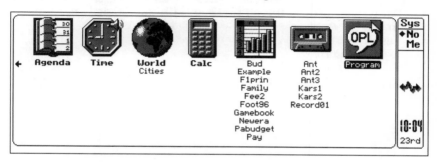

Memory Bar

On the right of the icon window is a window containing the words System, Normal and Memory. In the bottom right-hand corner the clock ticks away! Normal and Memory are options which are selected by pressing the ♦ key. Many Psion Series 3 applications have these options and their nature is such that you can only select one at a time. In this case it is simply a choice of having the Memory graphically displayed at the bottom of the System screen or not (see pictures over the page). Alternatively press the Menu key and you'll see that a ♦ menu is the last menu in the top right-hand corner. This menu corresponds to the ♦ key choice.

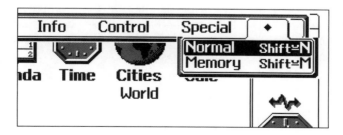

Press the ◆ key to see the Memory used/Free bar at the bottom of the screen. The significance of the numbers given here will be discussed later. The shaded part of the bar on the left indicates the proportion of the total memory in your Psion Series 3 which is in use. The empty part of the bar indicates the proportion of the total memory in your Psion Series 3 still unused (free). This is a handy view of the state of play in your Psion Series 3.

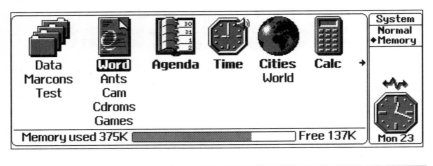

More to Come

You've now had a brief glimpse of the System menus and we'll return to them later in different contexts as we operate on files, set up the Psion Series 3, link to a PC and various other activities which revolve around the System environment. If you're finding it a bit daunting at the moment, don't worry. Keep trying the examples in this book and the principles will become clear. You can then apply these principles whenever you use your Psion Series 3 because it responds in a consistent fashion.

Chapter 3

....

Managing by Menus

You've encountered some menus already in the System screen. Menus are how you make your Psion Series 3 do what you want it to. In this chapter we'll look at how menus work and at some of the functions which are grouped in them and which many of the Psion Series 3 applications (such as Word and Data) have in common. If you master the use of these common menu items then you'll be some way towards mastering the use of your Psion. By the way, the Menu button is on the bottom row, on the left-hand side of the space bar.

Press the System icon to make sure you are in the System screen. Press Menu and the File tab (the bit shaped like the top of a file) appears with its menu options listed below. Press Menu again and the Disk tab and list appear. Continue pressing Menu to move to menus further to the right. Hold down the Shift key and press Menu to move to menus on the left. Press Menu with your left hand and press '9' with your right to see the ♦ menu pop up. Try pressing Menu in combination with other number keys to choose the different menus from left to right (1 to 9).

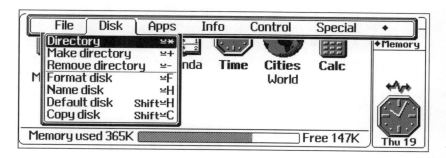

When a menu is displayed you can press the arrow keys to move the highlight up and down the list of functions. If you are at the top of the list and you press the up arrow key then the highlight will flip round to the bottom of the list. Use the down arrow key to return to the top! You can also use the Control key with the up/down arrow keys to move between top and bottom entries.

You can see the hot-key combination displayed alongside each function. Press the hot-key character without pressing the Psion key to highlight that menu option. Try it now. Press Menu to display the File menu, now press T to highlight the File attributes option. Pressing Enter will now activate this option. So pressing T and Enter is the equivalent of the hot-key press ∪T.

Press Esc to close any open menu list or dialogue box. Now press Menu again to display the list again. You'll notice that the last menu option you were using is highlighted. This is very useful if a menu item is often in use but you can't remember the hot-key. By pressing Menu it's likely you'll be presented with the regularly used item highlighted and ready to go. So, if System/File/Rename file was your last menu choice, that's where you'll return after pressing the Menu key.

Starting Up

If you have just started an application, the first menu – usually File/New file (∪N) – will be displayed. To demonstrate this, press the Word icon to open the Word application. Now press Menu and press Menu a second time to move to the next menu to the right of the one first displayed. Use the arrow keys to move left and right along the list.

An handy tip is to use the left arrow key to move from the first (File) menu to the last, which is the Special menu. It's a quick way to get to the Special menu options and is especially useful for a quick exit (∪X) – which appears at the bottom of the Special menu list.

The following menu descriptions relate mainly to the applications such as Sheet, Data, Word and Agenda. Press the Word icon to open Word so that you can check the menu lists as we go through the groupings.

Menu Groups

The functions you can carry out in an application are generally grouped in similar fashion so that they become familiar whichever application you are using. The File menu list contains operations to create a file and to update it (save), grouped with other related tasks such as merging files (combining into one), tidying and compressing files (making smaller) and reverting (going back) to an earlier version of a file.

Edit Menu

The next menu, Editing, is about working on the information in the applications, often in relation to moving it about and changing it. Hence under Edit in the menu bar you'll find Insert text and Copy text which, between them, can move text from one place to another, reproduce it in another place and delete it if required.

Copy in fact is the first operation followed by Insert. This is an important operation to be able to carry out and it's covered in full in the chapters on Word. You'll use it wherever you need to get text into the Psion Series 3.

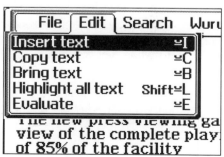

Bring text and Evaluate are also found under Edit. The first brings text in from other applications. You have to send it previously. Evaluate looks at numbers in the text and does a calculation for you. This can be quicker or more appropriate than using the calculator. Other actions to change things are also grouped here, such as changing entry details in Agenda and Calc and Undo in Sheet.

Finding Things

One of the things your Psion Series 3 is very good at is searching out information. Over time you'll enter more than you can imagine in the form of names and addresses, budgets, diary dates etc etc. That's why we'll look in depth at keeping that data safe through good practice. But what about finding what you're looking for?

The next menu along is Search, which contains different types of operation to 'find' text in the document you're working on. The dialogue for each application is different, reflecting the type of information involved. In Data you search for text and the result of the search is a card which contains the text so the Search menu has options to Find Previous and Find next so you can move around the cards.

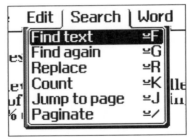

Word, on the other hand, has a Find and Replace dialogue box which includes a Case sensitive option. This means that it will find and replace a word or phrase irrespective of whether it's been written with a capital letter or not. Count, Jump to page and Paginate are also grouped here as vaguely related operations. Agenda groups Jump to date and Calendar and the Agenda-specific Find next overlap and View all repeats. You can see how you can make an informed guess as to where you'll find a particular menu and menu function in any application.

Also common to the applications are the last two menus on the list – and therefore on the far right of the menu bar – Special and ◆.

Special is important in the System screen but in fact, despite the name, in other applications it contains some rather ordinary functions. Printing matters come under this heading and also screen display. and Exit.

Special Settings

We'll deal with the printing aspects of Special in its own chapter but let's tackle the screen display aspects head on. Zoom in and Zoom out move in different directions through four 'zoom levels' on the text display. If you use a camera then I imagine you'll be familiar with the concept. Hold down the ∪ key and press Z four times in succession and you'll see the four different sizes of text which you can view.

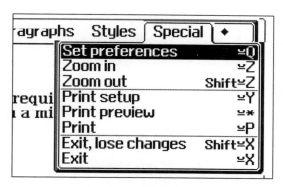

The zoom level doesn't change the information in your Psion Series 3. If you enter a lot of notes in a Database card in zoom level 1 and then change to zoom level 4, don't panic. The information you entered is still there but it isn't immediately displayed on screen. The text has been magnified and so takes up more room on the screen.

Use the arrow keys to scroll (move) down to the other lines of text which are below. Of course, this brings up the question of which zoom view you like to use and how this affects the design of, for example, your Data cards.

Zoom level	Lines available
Zoom level 1	13 lines
Zoom level 2	10 lines
Zoom level 3	9 lines
Zoom level 4	7 lines

Table 3.1. Lines in view in Database.

If you intend to work wholly, or mainly, in a particular zoom level then design your cards, spreadsheets and so on for your own convenience. This can become restrictive in the case of, for instance, a Word document, which needs to have lines, say, 50 characters long. In this sort of situation you'll have to use a lower level of zoom to view the whole line or get used to scrolling around the document.

Menu Matters

You've got the idea. Menus provide the means to operate the applications, which have many operations in common, so they are easy to find and use. It's time now to use one of these applications and the files it creates.

Chapter 4

••

Applications
and Files

 It's time to use an application and to work on the files it creates. As stated in the last chapter, Psion Series 3 applications work in similar ways to make it easier for you. When we get to later chapters which go into detail about each application, I'll point out when you need to be aware of the subtle differences and when you need to use a variation on a theme. For now, it's a matter of getting to grips with some basics.

First off we'll create a document and a file. Press the Sheet icon and the spreadsheet page with columns and rows appears. We'll look at spreadsheet work in detail later but in the meantime we need our practice file. Follow this PsiGuide to create one.

PsiGuide begins... Creating test file in Sheet

Type in:

per hour

and press the Tab key to move the text cursor to the next box to the right. In spreadsheets this box is known as a 'cell'. It can contain text or numbers. Type

hours

and press Tab, type

fee

File	Edit	View	Search
1 per hour	hours	fee	
2 35	2	70	
3			
4			
5			
6			
7			

and press Enter. Use the arrow keys to move the cursor back to the cell A2, that is column A, row 2. This is how you refer to cells, by their grid co-ordinate, a bit like reading a map. The A2 is displayed in the top left-hand corner of the screen.

Now type

35

press Tab, type

2

press Tab, type

*=A2*B2*

and press Enter.

PsiGuide ends...

The asterisk (*) character is the multiplication sign on your Psion Series 3. This little multiplication A2*B2 at the end gives you an idea of what a spreadsheet is all about. There are no numbers in the formula but only references to other cells – A2 and B2 – and the values these cells contain. You can vary these values. For instance, if you decide to put up your hourly rate, you increase the number in A2, for example to 40. This action will be reflected in both A2 and in C2, which is the cell with the formula (=A2*B2) which refers to it.

Save Example

We've done some work so let's save it, for safety in case we make an error and wish to revert to our current situation and in case something untoward occurs to cause the loss of our data (very rare). This file is also going to serve as an example file we can work on from the System screen. Press Menu and choose Save As (∪S). A dialogue box pops up with a blank space for you to type a name for your spreadsheet. 'Fee' seems an appropriate name so type it in, press Enter and

Saving as Fee

will appear briefly in the bottom right-hand corner of the display.

Watch Out

At this point I want to explain something a bit strange about Psion applications. You have now clearly saved a file called 'Fee' onto the internal disk. It said so in the dialogue box. And the information on the screen you are looking at is in that file. However the spreadsheet you are working on now is not 'Fee'. It's still 'Sheet', which is the default filename given to your document when you first pressed on the Sheet icon. The big problem with this is that, if you don't realise what's happened, you are liable to save into the wrong file. There is a special danger when you've amended a file, save as under a new name and then proceed to adjust it again, then save onto your original file.

To prove the point, move to cell D1 in your mini spreadsheet and type

new file

press Menu and choose Save (∪S). When you examine the Fee file in a moment you'll *not* find this new entry – it's only now in the Sheet file.

Press the System icon to get to the System display, use the arrow keys to bring the Sheet icon into view and to highlight 'Fee', which will appear in a list underneath the Sheet icon. When 'Fee' is highlighted, press Enter. You are now in the Fee document and using Save (∪S) will save changes automatically into this file. The separate file Sheet remains untouched.

You've now discovered that the information in your Psion Series 3 can be stored in individually named files and, in order to change the data in any such file, it has to be worked on in an application, such as we have just done in Sheet application.

I got you into all this because I think it's a potential difficulty you'll face when you jump into an application and save new data into a file. There are two ways around the problem. The first, unnatural, approach is to take action to create a file as soon as you enter an application. This means not working on the default file at all. 'Default' by the way is what you get when the you don't explicitly tell the computer what you want.

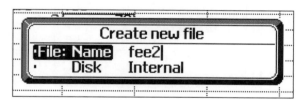

When you enter Sheet, don't start typing. Instead press Menu, choose New file and type the name of your new file in the Create new file dialogue. When you do this from scratch, there is no confusion as where the next Save is going to. Give it a try now. Choose File/New file, type in

Dummy

and press Enter.

A message

Filename Created

will flash up in the bottom right-hand corner.

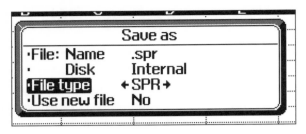

The second, and recommended, method is to make full use of the Save as dialogue. The last item in the dialogue reads Use new file. Move to it with the arrow keys and choose Yes. After the file is saved, Sheet will leave you editing that file, not the 'default' as described above.

Leaving the Scene

Another aspect of a Sheet document you might like to think about for a moment is the lack of a 'close document' option on the File menu.

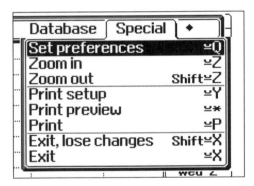

We've finished creating our Fee document and we've saved it. So leave the document now via the Special/Exit (⊍X) menu option or Exit, lose changes (Shift⊍X) if you don't want to save the changes you've made since your last save. Press the left arrow key once to move from the File menu to the Special menu.

This Exit, lose changes option is useful if you've saved your document, tried something in your spreadsheet and got in a mess and wish to get out of it without saving the mess to the file. The File/Revert (⊍V) option similarly gets you back to the position you were in when you last saved a file. This is only possible because the document in the application and the document in the file are separate entities as proved by our experiments earlier.

File Operations

You've now created a document in an application and you've saved it as a file. You've also learned how to distinguish between the document, which is in the application, and the file, which is a version of the document saved on the disk. You'll be doing a lot of work on documents in the different Psion applications later in the book and you'll create many files.

You can perform file management operations, such as copy and rename, on these files from the System screen. That's what we'll be doing in the next chapter.

Chapter 4

....

File
Management

 Some of the Psion applications have already got their own files when you turn on. When you first open the System screen you'll see the Data icon and beneath it is listed just one file 'Data'. This is the standard or 'default' file. It doesn't mean you *have* to use this file. You can create new files to hold the record cards with information you type into the Data application, and in later chapters that's one of the things we'll do. In the meantime Data needs something to work with and the Data file is it.

When you save a file from an application, it appears in a list beneath the application icon on the System screen. Later we'll look at how the files you have created are stored and at a different way of working on them but for now let's stick with the System screen. After all Psion has made things easy for us, so let's use the facilities!

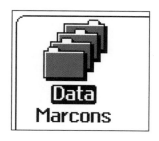

Files appear listed beneath their application. An open file is shown in bold and highlighted at the top. The others follow in alphabetical order.

Most of your file management will take place on the System screen, operating on the files which appear beneath the application icons there. You can only use a System menu function, Rename for instance, on a file name which is highlighted.

The first thing to try then is to use the arrow keys to move left and right along the top row of file names and up and down individual file lists to highlight the file name of your choice. Seek out the Sheet file name. Use another file name if you wish, such as the Fee file we saved in the last chapter. Make sure the file name you are going to operate on is highlighted.

File-Related Menus

At this point I'll go through the different file-related menu functions to explain what they do and you can use the filename you've highlighted to experiment on as we go. The functions are activated in the ways we have discussed in previous chapters, by choosing them from a menu – activated by pressing the Menu button – or by pressing the appropriate hot-key.

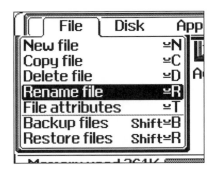

If you're game, now is the time to start to use the hot-key combinations. Occasionally you'll press the wrong keys but just use the Esc key to get out and try again or use Menu to check the correct key combination. The more you do it, the better you'll get and the more time you'll save in the long run

New file

First up in the File menu is New file, which creates a file under the name you type into the dialogue box. Because you have highlighted a file name which is listed beneath Sheet on the System screen, you are presented with a Create new "Sheet" file dialogue and the new file will be a Sheet type. If the file name you had highlighted on the System screen was listed beneath Data then you would be offered a Create new "Data" file dialogue, which would create a file of this type.

The files which each application creates are very different because of the nature of the information in them. The Word file has text plus formatting commands for instance and the Sheet file has text, number values and formulae to store. Because of their particular nature, you can't create your own files for Time or for Calc. These applications work with information which is internal to them and not available for editing.

Copy file

Copy file is for making a copy of a file. It makes a duplicate under the same name or under another name. The From file: Name line shows the name of the file to copy. It can be changed with the arrow keys. The To file: Name line is where you enter the name of the new file which the copy process will create. If you are copying to the same disk, eg Internal disk to Internal disk, then you *must* type in a different name in the To file: Name line. The filing system can't cope with two files of the same name in the same place. If you are making the copy on a different disk, eg Internal disk to disk A then you can type in the same name in the To file: Name line. A file of the same name on a different disk doesn't confuse the filing system.

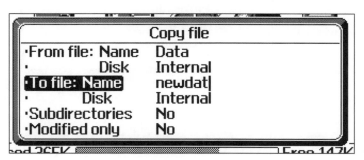

The To file: Disk line shows Internal if you've come from the System screen but using the arrow keys you can select other disks by their names, eg A, B, C, which are names of external disks, if you have them present in your Psion Series 3. If the disks aren't actually there, although you can select them, you can't then do anything else in the dialogue. You have to reselect a disk which is actually present. In a standard Psion Series 3 the only disk available is the internal disk.

The Copy dialogue box also contains Subdirectories and Modified only options, which are Yes/No settings. Use the arrow keys to choose between them. We'll look at file structures, including subdirectories in the chapter on the Filing System. Modified is an attribute of a file connected with file backup – see Attributes below. This option allows you to copy only modified files as part of a backing-up process, thus saving time by making copies of only those files which have changed since the last backup.

Copy is useful if you have a file which you want to use as the basis of a new file. Just copy it under a new name and then edit it. In this way standard letters , invoices, or spreadsheet formulae can be edited and re-used instead of retyping information from scratch. Copy can't be used with Agenda and Data files to duplicate them successfully. To create a new identical file for these applications you have to load the file and use Save as, entering a new name for the file as you do so.

Delete file

Next is Delete file, dangerous but straightforward. Choosing any of these menu options generates a dialogue box for you to fill in the details so there's always the chance to check what you are doing before putting it into action, particularly important in the case of delete when it's always best to have a chance to think again. Delete is irreversible. Once the file has been deleted, it's gone for good.

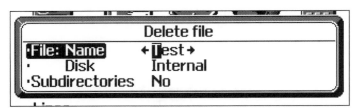

The dialogue box's first entry is File: Name and this initially contains the name of the file which is highlighted on the System screen. This is the file which will be deleted. Press Enter and the deed is done! If you wish to select a different file then use the arrow keys to display other file names. When the right file name comes into view, press Enter to delete it.

Rename file

Rename has the simple purpose of giving you a chance to rethink the name of a file.

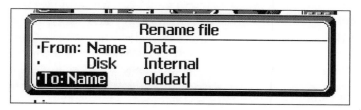

You may wish to make a file name more appropriate or bring it into line with a naming system you've devised for your files. I'll offer some advice on naming conventions at the end of this chapter.

Attributes

File attributes (∪T) gives some basic information about the file and provides options to change the *status* of the file – what you can and can't do to it .

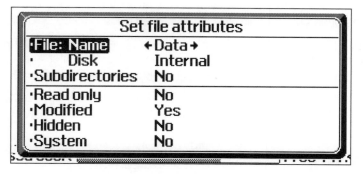

Once you are in the dialogue box, you are not restricted to the file name which is in the top line. You can use the arrow keys to choose any other file from the list in which your highlighted file name resides. For instance the file name Fee is listed beneath the Sheet icon. With Fee highlighted, the other file names listed beneath Sheet will appear in the dialogue when you press the arrow keys.

The subdirectories entry is irrelevant in this dialogue with Yes/No settings making no difference in this context. The Read only line is a very important protection which you can apply to a file if you feel that it shouldn't be changed in any way. Set it to Yes to protect it from change.

If you try to save such a file after Read only has been set to Yes, then the

not changed

message will appear and the file will remain the same. However you will still be able to rname, delete or copy the file.

You can't perform filing operations on files which are in use. Often files are opened inside applications even though you are not working directly on them but are in the System screen. If you get the message

Error Rename "whatever"

File or device in use

Abandon	**Skip**	**Retry**
Esc	**Space**	**Enter**

you are probably trying to rename a file which is open and 'in use' inside an application. You'll have to go into the application and choose exit from the Special menu. Then you can go back to your filing operation.

The Modified line (also called a field) of the Attributes dialogue box tells you if the file has been changed since you last carried out a backup operation.

The Hidden field is usually set to 'no' but if you want to get a file off the System screen then this is how to do it. Choose Yes and press Enter and the file will no longer be displayed in the list beneath its icon on the System screen.

The file is only hidden, not deleted. It remains in the appropriate directory in the underlying filing system and can be resurrected – see Chapter 14 on the Filing System for more details.

Trying Out

At this point you should start to have an idea of how things work, so let's run through a few of the filing activities again. Press System and use the arrow keys to locate the Sheet icon, highlighting the file name 'Fee'. Press Menu and choose File/Rename. Then type in 'Fee2' as your new name. Watch it change in the list of file names beneath Sheet on the System screen. Choose Copy and give it the To file: Name 'Dummy'. This file name will now appear in the list of file names underneath Sheet. Use the arrow keys to highlight Dummy and press Menu again, choose Delete (∪D) and say goodbye to Dummy.

Note that the file which is open in Sheet, appears first in the file list beneath the icon. The other files are listed in alphabetical order. When you exit from a document, its filename drops back into its place in the alphabetical list. If there are too many files for the display, those at the bottom disappear. To view these files use the arrow keys to move down. When the cursor moves off the bottom of the screen, the next file in the list scrolls (moves) up into view while the first entry at the top of the list disappears. Using the up arrow key again brings the first few files back into view.

With the Fee2 file name highlighted, press the Delete key. There is no delete dialogue but, perhaps surprisingly, a message

Fee2 is not running

will appear. Now press Enter to open Fee2 and the worksheet will appear. Press the System icon to return to the System screen and you'll find Fee2 highlighted at the top of the list beneath the Sheet icon. It's at the top because it's still open (you didn't Exit from it, did you?). Now press the Delete key and you'll get an

Exit "Fee2"?

No/Yes dialogue. This is the quick way to Exit (⊙X) an open application from the System screen. But be careful because it does save changes you've made since the last save. If you want to 'Exit, lose changes' (Shift⊙X) then you'll need to go into the open application and choose 'Exit, lose changes' from the Special menu.

Now use the arrow keys to move to another file in the list – use Sheet if you haven't got any others. Press Enter when the file is highlighted. A message

Fee2 is busy

is displayed. This is because normally you can only open one file at a time and Fee2 is already using this slot. Now hold down the Shift key and press Enter. This opens the new file without complaint. You've now got two files open, both in Sheet, and you can switch between them via the System menu.

File Naming

When you give a file a name it's worth spending a few seconds devising a sensible, memorable, name and one which is consistent with other names you have used or intend to use in the future. This will make it easier to distinguish files for backing up, archiving (long-term storage) and deletion. Unless you've got a top of the range Psion Series 3 you'll find storage space is at a premium so deleting old files is important. More of this in the Filing System chapter.

Files are already grouped by application category for you so you don't have to worry about what application type they are. However, you may wish to devise your own abbreviations to distinguish between different categories of file, for instance between work and personal files.

Info Menu

If you want to know how much space you've got on your disk(s) then Disk info is available (∪K) from the Info menu on the System screen.

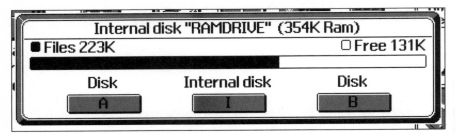

Press either A, I or B to make a selection from the available disks. If the disk isn't physically present, the dialogue says so. Note that the internal disk is also referred to as RAMDRIVE.

The Info menu also tells you how your batteries are standing the strain and other information about the Psion Series 3 you are using.

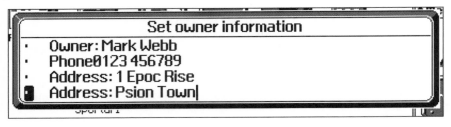

Set owner (∪P) is where you type in your details in case your Psion Series 3 goes missing although I feel the odds against another Psion owner finding your computer and knowing how to get this information may be high.

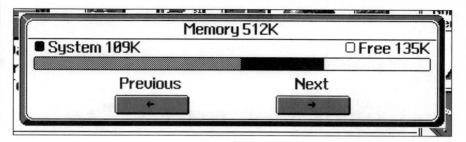

Memory info (∪M) may also be turned on by choosing Memory with the ♦ key on the System screen.

This option will display the Memory used/free bar and two Previous and Next buttons (activated by the left and right arrow keys) which display individual memory usage for the system software and open applications, including the disks. Press the arrow keys to view these displays.

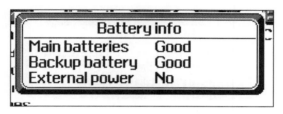

Battery info (∪B) displays the condition of the Main batteries, Backup battery and External power (No unless a mains power unit is in use).

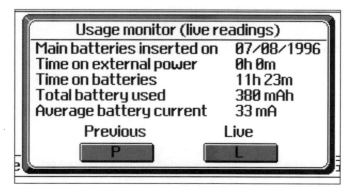

The Usage monitor (∪U) allows you to check closely the performance of the batteries you use in your Psion Series 3. It displays the 'live' ie current readings with an option to look back at the performance of the batteries previously installed.

About Series 3 (∪V) displays the version number of the software which you should quote if you have a technical problem and need to ask Psion or a Psion dealer what to do.

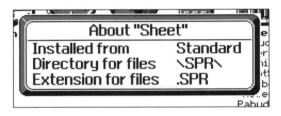

About application (Shift∪V) gives three details about the application currently highlighted. Installed from is Standard for a built-in application, e.g. Sheet as shown above. If the application has been installed from a Psion disk or from a PC then this setting changes.

The Directory for files and Extension for files is handy information for advanced file management – see Chapter 14 . Each application saves its files by default into the Directory for files for that application. The files can subsequently be moved to other disks or directories. For example, the \SPR\ directory shown above is the directory for spreadsheets saved from Sheet.

When you save from an application you give your work a file name. The application then adds its own three character extension to the file name. The file name and extension are separated by a full stop. The .SPR extension shown above is the extension for spreadsheets saved from Sheet. Other extensions distinguish files for Word, Data, ASCII etc. These extensions are useful when searching for files of a particular type and are used by applications such as PsiWin when they transfer, and optionally convert, files to other system types.

Chapter 6

Globe Trotting

The Psion Series 3 is fully portable and entirely capable of travelling the world, crossing datelines and moving between time zones with the most travelled of international business person or holiday-maker.

In the next three chapters we'll move rapidly through time. No, this is not H.G. Wells, but the time machine called Psion Series 3. The World and Time functions place your Psion Series 3 in time and space so that the other applications, especially Agenda, can manage time on your behalf.

In chapters six and seven we'll look at how to make the correct settings in World and Time, how to create some pretty alarming alarm calls and how to make your international calls from the Psion Series 3. Then, having synchronised watches, we'll move on in chapter eight to Agenda and its many time management functions.

In the beginning is the World. Like its users, the Psion Series 3 is international in its outlook. The World application is where you tell the Psion Series 3 where it's currently located and what time it is. Choose World from the System screen or press the World icon the front of the Psion Series 3 if World is already running.

World Affair

In the middle of your screen appears a conventional map of the world, which is pretty but doesn't really do much. On the right is information about the Home city and country which you'll probably find displays London inner, with United Kingdom below it. Above is a clock with today's date and time – in London inner anyway – and above the clock the sunrise and sunset times are given.

In the middle, below the map is a telephone number and a distance in miles. The telephone number is in fact a prefix number with international dialling code from the home country, dialling prefix for the country listed on the left and dialling prefix for the city listed on the left. The distance is between the Home city and the City city. On the left then we have a symmetrical display with clock and sunrise/sunset but the big difference is we can change the selected country and city.

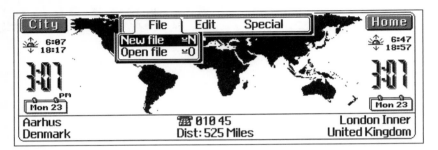

To change this you need to choose from the list of cities and countries which your Psion Series 3 holds already stored in its memory or you need to add to this list yourself. Alternatively you could edit an existing entry although this is less desirable because you never know when Kuala Lumpar or London outer might come handy.

Quick Check

The quick way to check if your own city – if you are a city dweller – is in the list is to make sure the left-hand entry is highlighted and type in the first few letters of the city name. The selected text will change as World tries to match your typed characters with a name in its list. It's not much help changing the country to your country first because the two lists work independently.

Let's say you've just landed at Köln/Bonn airport to visit your German office. In the bus or taxi to your hotel you can change the left-hand display by typing in 'col' to get Cologne. The country changes to Germany automatically and the other information changes with it. The City is now set to Cologne and Home is still London. If it's a short stay you may wish to leave it that way so that you've got local time information to hand. However your Psion Series 3 is still 'home' in London.

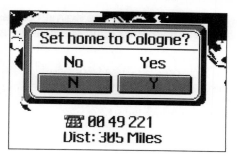

To make Cologne 'home', however temporarily, choose Special/Set home city (⌣H). Type 'Y' when prompted Yes/No and the right-hand display changes to Cologne. The left-hand side retains Cologne also and you may wish to select your 'real' home city here so that you've got local time information here (for ringing home for instance). It's also ready to be transferred over to the right-hand side again when you land back at your home airport.

'Phone Home

If you do not dwell in a major city then don't worry, you can easily create a new entry for your home town. The main reason for doing this is to have your home telephone code set up. Other Psion Series 3 applications can use this number to dial home accurately.

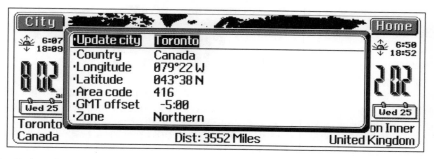

The Psion Series 3 does this by sending the national and town prefix numbers, followed by the local number – usually stored in Data or Agenda. See the chapters on these applications for further details. No physical connection with the phone is required because the Psion Series 3 generates a sound for each number which a tone-dialled telephone will recognise. Just hold the Psion Series 3's speaker (on the bottom) next to the mouthpiece of the telephone before dialling (⌣Help).

It's pretty important then to have the correct dialling prefixes entered into your city entry. This gives us an opportunity to edit a city entry and to enter one of our own.

First, let's play a little trick on ourselves. Choose Update city from the Edit menu. Change the entry and press Enter. You'll get the error message:

Add/update London Inner failed

Invalid name

Continue

Esc

You get a similar (Modify United Kingdom failed) message if you try to Update country. The reason for this is that World is getting the city information from a file (information grouped in memory) which is read only and you can't change this type of memory storage. The way around this is provided by World itself.

Go to the file menu and create a new file – New file (∪N) with a name – say 'cities'. Choose your own to suit.

Any changes or additions you make in World will be saved into this file and, while World remains active, will stay as part of the cities list. If you leave World by choosing Special/Exit (∪X) then when you next enter World you'll need to do so via the Cities file, which is now listed underneath the World application on the System screen.

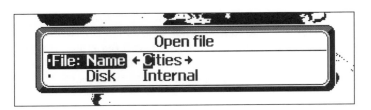

If you get into World via the World file, then you'll discover that any updates you have made in the Cities file are not available but you're back with the *original* City information. In this case you can Open file (∪O) and choose the 'Cities' file to get updated again. We've run through this concept before, of having more than one file available to an application. If you have more than one additional file for World, then make sure that you keep track of *where* you are making your changes.

New Numbers

To edit a city entry use Update city and type in new information before pressing Enter.

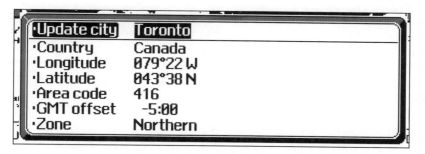

On my Psion Series 3 the UK city telephone codes have not been updated and appear to have missed Telephone Day completely. I believe there's an application to update files by putting in the extra '1' but it's easy enough to do this manually in World. Clearly if you have large Data files containing telephone numbers then you'll need an application to speed things up.

·Update	Canada
·Capital city	Ottawa
·National code	1
·National prefix	1
·International prefix	011
·GMT offset	-5:00
·Zone	Northern

Similarly the international dialling prefix for the UK hasn't changed in my Psion Series 3 from 010 to 00. It changed to come into line with the European version. Use Update country for this sort of thing.

Adding Your Home Town

OK, that's the editing part, what about adding your own city, or home town?

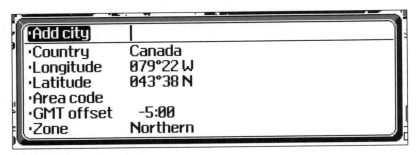

The option Add city (⌐A) pops up a dialogue based on the country currently listed on the left-hand side. With you country in the left-hand side and highlighted, press ⌐A and type in the city name in the top line of the dialogue. If you don't use your home country as a basis of your entry you'll need to check that the GMT (Greenwich Mean Time) offset is correct. The most difficult entry is the longitude and latitude of your city – the sort of information you don't normally carry about with you – do you?

When you've entered all the information you can, press Enter and you are given the opportunity to 'place' your city on the map. You could really have fun with a friend's Psion Series 3 here, putting London inner into the Pacific Ocean for instance. But, staying serious, this is an imprecise method of locating your city but better than nothing until you can look up the longitude and latitude in your atlas. Move the arrow keys to position the flashing cursor as best you can. The distance and sunrise/set will not be accurate until you type in the correct details. Use Update city (⌐U) later to do this.

Well that covers the main setting-up functions in World. There are a few menu options not covered above so let's have a quick look at them below before we move on to Time in the next chapter.

Other Options

Unless you want to free space, there's no great joy in using Delete city en masse. For individual entries, use Update to make sure they contain the right information.

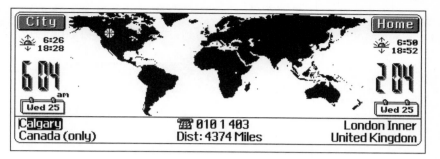

Current country only (∪L) restricts the left-hand display to cities in the country defined by the country showing in the left-hand display when this choice is made. It's handy for cutting down the options if you've got a really huge list but, with the standard list, I've found it unnecessary.

In addition to Set home city and Exit, the Special menu lets you define the units of distance from miles, km and nautical miles – on that cruise you've promised yourself. Digital/analog clocks can also be toggled (switched between) with ∪C. Personally I find the Analog setting the easier to use. The digital read-out clashes with the many other numbers on the World screen.

Chapter 7

Hands of Time

 Time waits for no-one! And the Psion Series 3 keeps time on your behalf but don't be too alarmed. As usual, you are in full control.

Hands revolve, bells chime, buzzers sound, clocks speak, the world awakes in successive waves as the sun tips over the horizon...

Wakey! wakey!

That's the sound to which I've recently been roused form my valuable slumber. it's the sound of two young children shouting 'wakey wakey'. but the children are usually still tucked up in their beds. It's their voices – recorded by the Psion Series 3 and played back through its speaker – which rough up my morning.

It's a combination of the clock/alarm function (Time) and the sound sampling function (Record) and it's all too effective! I'm sure you can think of your own application of this combination. You needn't worry about the sound sampling bit if you're happy to just have rings, chimes, fanfares, softbells or church bells, all of which are already residing in your Psion Series 3 ready to pounce on your eardrums.

Setting Time

Because the Psion Series 3 assumes you are going to use it for things like personal time management (like getting up in the morning), the Time function, though simple, is directly relevant to alarms/reminders and the diary features of Agenda.

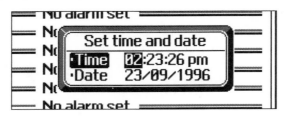

It's sensible to have the correct time set and this is done from the Setting/Time and date menu (∪T). A dialogue appears and you can set the time and date by typing in to the highlighted blocks and using the arrow keys to move around, finishing off with Enter.

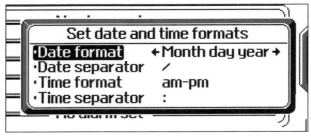

The format of this entry dialogue and of other time displays is controlled from the (∪F) Formats menu. This dialogue offers:

Day month year

Year month day

Month day year

formats. You can choose the date separator (default /) by typing in a character from the keyboard, but not a-z or 0-9. The Time format can be

am-pm

24 hour

and the time separator can also be changed (default :).

Once you've made your format selection, this will be used by all applications to present time and date information. Try it. Make a change and then go into Agenda and press ∪J to jump to a date. The date format will be the one you've chosen in Time.

Summer Time

Time is relative so it's easy for us humans to mess around with it. Hence we can change our clocks around at certain times of the year to suit our lifestyles.

The Set summer times dialogue (∪S) offers

  Home is On/Off

  European is On/Off

  Northern is On/Off

  Southern is On/Off

Home and Away

The Home city option (∪H) means you can choose from the World list of cities (see previous chapter) so that Time starts with the correct information about the region it's in.

If you've created a new World file to update or add cities then you'll not be able to use it from here but instead should ensure that World is properly set up.

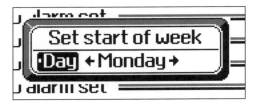

Start of week (∪B) is an interesting menu option. The concepts of 'weekend', 'back to work on Monday' and even 'rest on the Sabbath/seventh day' etc are not universal so this can be used to tell the Psion Series 3 where to begin. Escape to leave, Enter to confirm.

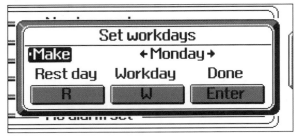

Workdays (∪W) brings up the Set workdays dialogue in which it's tempting to include only a couple of days at the most. Use the arrow keys to scroll through each day in turn and to set it as a Rest day (R) or Workday (W). Press Enter when done.

Alarms

Alarms can be set from Time and from Agenda. If you just want an alarm as a reminder then it's quicker to do it from Time.

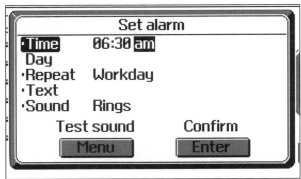

Set alarm (∪T or press Enter or Tab) brings up a dialogue which will become very familiar as you use Time and, over the next few chapters, Agenda. Type in the time for the alarm, using the arrow keys to move up and down the entries. Repeat offers these options, including Workday which relates to the choices made previously in the Settings menu:

Once

Weekly

Workday

Daily

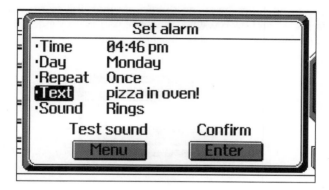

You can type in a text message, making this a great way of leaving a message to a colleague or family member. Set the time so that the alarm will go off when you know the receiver will be in the room, type in your message and then leave the Psion Series 3 in a prominent, or previously agreed, position. The receiver can either read the message on turning on the Psion Series 3 or will be reminded to do so by the alarm going off.

Sound is where you choose the kind of noise your alarm will make, as mentioned at the start of this chapter. See the chapter on sound sampling with Record if you want to leave sound messages or to make your alarms more personal. The sound of an oncoming vehicle should wake someone up!

'Happy Birthday' always goes down well, providing you've got the right day although Agenda should sort that our for you. The fanfare always sounds as though the cavalry is coming and is therefore my favourite. Test the sounds out for yourself by pressing Menu.

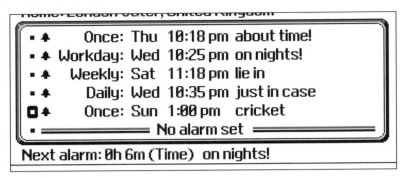

When set, the alarm appears in the Time display. A bell icon is followed by the type of alarm you have set, plus the details of when the alarm will occur and finally the text message which will be shown. If you set a Workday repeat on a Restday then the alarm will occur on the next Workday. Use the arrow keys to move up and down the list of alarms.

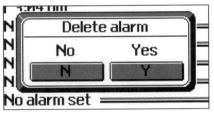

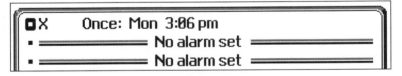

The Delete (◡D or Delete key) and Disable alarm (◡-) options work on the selected alarm entry. Delete removes the alarm settings completely while Disable replaces the bell icon with an X character to indicate that it is suspended until Enable alarm is used (◡-).

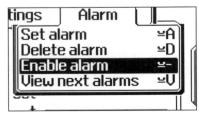

View next alarms (∪V) brings up full information about the next alarms, how long to go and exactly when, and the text attached. Enter moves through each alarm in turn.

Going Off

When the alarm goes off you have to respond by pressing Esc to turn off, space bar to make the alarm 'snooze' for five minutes before going off again, Enter to silence the alarm pending your decision to remove it.

Keep hitting the space bar to add five minutes each press to the snooze time, up to 60 minutes longer in bed!

If you don't want your alarm to interrupt a meeting – or quiet romantic evening if you're lucky – then, when you are in the System screen, press ∪S and set All sound to Off.

Chapter 8

On the Agenda

 Your Psion Series 3 packs a lot into a pocket-size computer. Although It's smaller than the average Filofax type diary/organiser of the leather and paper kind, it manages to provide one of these in addition to its many other productivity tools.

The big three applications on any desktop computer are wordprocessor, spreadsheet and database. On any portable computer the new recruit at the top table is the personal information manager (PIM), the digital version of the personal organiser but with the big difference that it doesn't damage your clothes as you cram it into your inadequate pockets!

On the Psion Series 3 the PIM is called Agenda and the program combines the functions of note-jotter, diary, appointments and time-manager. There's much speculative talk about computer software which will, in the future, organise your appointments for you, or at least calculate the best 'window' for you and your colleagues to meet. In the meantime you'll have to manage your own affairs and Agenda can help you do that in many different ways through its timed entries, memos and to-do lists. Like all PIMs, Agenda requires your commitment to its regular use, otherwise you don't get the benefit. It needn't rule your life but daily checking is recommended during periods of work.

Opening Up

When you press the Agenda icon for the first time, you enter the System screen with the word Agenda highlighted beneath the icon on screen. Press Enter to open the file called Agenda in the program Agenda. Later you'll find that the program Agenda can save and open files under other names if you wish.

You'll see

Opening Agenda

and

Agenda opened

messages and the main Agenda screen with a page looking like the page of a ringbound diary with lines underlining each hour between the hours of 6 in the morning to 10 in the evening. We've already encountered the way that your Psion Series 3 handles time and Agenda conforms to the same principles.

Take a look at the window on the right-hand side of the main window and you'll see a long list of ♦ selections. As usual pressing the ♦ key selects one of the options listed here. Try it now and you'll see, in turn, the Day, Week, Year, To-do, Anniv(ersary) and List 'views' of Agenda. The corresponding hot-keys are Day (Shift∪D), Week (Shift∪W), Year (Shift∪Y), To-do (Shift∪T), Anniv(ersary) (Shift∪A) and List (Shift∪L).

The 'view' is a way of displaying the information which you enter into Agenda and each view is appropriate to a particular situation. Day view is good for making entries, Week view is good for checking your diary for the coming week, To-do view is a 'get busy' list and Anniversary view reminds you of those important personal dates.

You can change the views which are available in the ♦list through choosing Set up ♦list (Shift∪♦) and selecting Yes/No for each entry. In this way you can restrict easy access to a particular list but it's not really a security feature, more a way of making the menu more usable. If you only use Week and To-do views then restrict the menu to these and you've the simplest, single key press, way of moving between them.

Entering Information

Don't get bogged down in the different types of entering information, not initially, even if they are imposed upon you. Make sure you are in the Day view. Use the right and left arrow keys to move the square block cursor to today's date and the up and down arrow keys to choose a position at the hour of your choice.

Press Enter to activate a flashing cursor and type in some text. Press Enter and the Day entry details dialogue pops up with Timed entry highlighted.

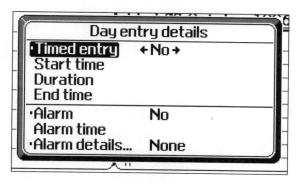

Use the arrow keys to choose No and press Enter to leave you with a simple note at the hour of the day you chose. This is Agenda at its simplest and you can use mini notes like these quite effectively as reminders. If you want to put in a substantial note then this becomes a memo, more of which below.

Once you've got an entry down, it's easy to amend any part of it. Head for the Edit menu:

to simply change the text in your entry.

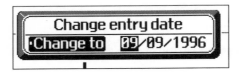

to amend the date when your plans change.

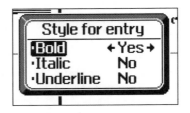

Or you can simply alter the appearance of the entry on screen to distinguish it in some way. You could make all your hair-dressing appointments bald, sorry bold!

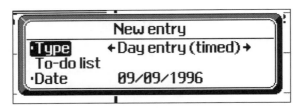

Your can also make a new entry from the Edit menu. This is necessary if you wish to create a To-do or repeating entry from scratch.

PsiGuide begins... Moving an Agenda entry

When you want to move an entry from one place to another, go to the entry using the arrow keys and choose Copy entry ((∧C). Note the date you are at and then use Jump to date (∧J) or the arrow keys to move to the new position at the new date of your choice.

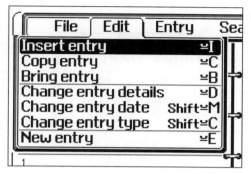

Now choose Insert entry (∧I) to place the entry at the new spot. Did you remember the date of the original entry? Use ∧J to move back to it. Highlight the entry and press the Delete key to remove it.

You can have more than one data file for Agenda. If you wish to move or copy an entry from one data file to another, open the first, use Copy entry (∧C), move to the second data file (from the System screen is easiest) and use Bring entry (∧B) to position it anew.

PsiGuide ends

Timed Entries

The 'default' in the Timed entry dialogue is Yes, which is the choice to make when you have are making an entry for a period of work, a visit or meeting.

Any entry can be turned into a Timed entry by moving the cursor to the entry and pressing Enter to bring up the dialogue, before changing the Timed entry field to Yes. The Start time for a Timed entry is filled in at the time you chose on the Day view and the default Duration is one hour. Make your changes by using the arrow keys and careful retyping.

The bottom panel in the dialogue deals with alarms. If you choose Alarm Yes then you need to complete the Alarm time, which will be previous to the Start time above it. The Alarm details... entry requires you to press the Tab key to bring up a sub-dialogue to set the exact time of the alarm in relation to the actual entry. Here too you can choose the sound for your Alarm and you can test it out.

Once you've confirmed the details of a timed entry, any text you've typed to go with your timed entry will appear in the Day view, and the List view, with an arrow and the end time after it in brackets.

Entry Icons

Once an entry has been assigned a property – such as an alarm – a little picture appears beside it.

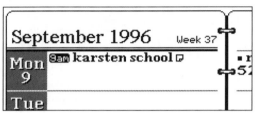

A bell indicates an alarm setting and a square with a corner 'folded' indicates a (paper) memo. These icons appear in Day view, Week view and List view.

Moving Around

If you want to place an entry some considerable time in advance or you want to check back on a memo, you'll need to find dates and times rapidly. Hot-keys can come in very handy or you can choose the equivalents from the Search menu in Agenda.

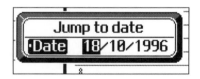

You can move to the previous entry with Shift⌣F and to the next entry with Shift⌣G. Jump to a particular date with ⌣J and move to a date via the Year View with Shift⌣J.

There are other methods you might wish to try. If the date's quite close then just keep you finger on the arrow keys to scroll quickly through the days.

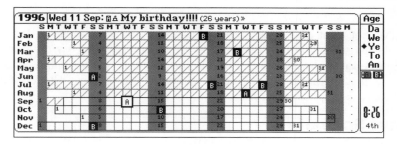

If the date is sometime away then it will be quicker to use the ◆ key to get the Year view and then use the arrow keys to move to the date and then ◆ again to return to Week or Day view. List view can be used in a similar manner to quickly scroll up or down the list to the required entry before flipping back into a Day or Week view.

List

List view is very useful because you can see all your entries by scrolling down through them. Pressing Enter over an entry allows you to edit it and change its nature. Today's date is emboldened and any outstanding To-do entries are highlighted.

To-do

If you want the To-do list then pressing the ◆ key or, much quicker, pressing Shift⌣T, will bring round that display.

You can give To-do entries different 'properties' which are appropriate to their status in your life. The Priority setting determines wherein the list this To-do is to come. Only priority 1 entries are displayed in the Agenda diary pages. A priority setting between 2 and 9 doesn't display except on the To-do list screen and here the lower the priority number the further up the list the entry comes.

To-do Types

To-do entries pop up every day until you delete them – either because you've done the job or you've given up and won't want to be reminded! All entries, timed or untimed, for the day are also displayed and remain until deleted even though the date has passed by. The display order is:

    To-do dated

    To-do undated

    Day entry timed

    Day entry untimed

If there's a long list then press Shift∪D to get the Day view.

If you've got a lot of To-dos coming through from previous dates then they push the timed day entries off the bottom of the Day view, which is a good reason to prioritise your To-dos. Put only the 'must do' entries in the display (1) category. If you want a list of To-dos you only have to press Shift∪T for the whole story.

Safari Scenario

I've introduced some of the features of Agenda. Now I'll take you through a little role-play in which you, the Psion Series 3-toting business person, plan your time around a well-earned holiday. After this I'll get down to detail with a run through the menus in Agenda.

Let's say that you are about to go on holiday and, on your return, you'll have a lot of catching up to do at work. You'll need to find out what's happening, revive the project you're working on – nothing will have been done in your absence – make sure the materials you need are to hand, and send details of the project to all your colleagues, inside and outside your organisation. First off you'll need to 'phone around to tell people you will be on holiday for a fortnight, and don't forget your close friend's birthday coming up during the two weeks you are away!

Agenda Test

The above list is probably less than you actually have to do in similar circumstances but this scenario will serve as a good test of Agenda.

The first thing to do is to itemise what you've got on your plate. When you press the Agenda icon you are offered a screen display which looks like a single day diary page. If the date for the page is wrong, ie not today's date, then press ∪J to go to today's date. You've now got today's diary page in front of you. We'll use the page as a notepad to jot down our list of things to do.

sort out
HA▸**send out project info**
HB **email timetable and deadlines**
BT plans to be completed by 3rd oct
BT checklist by 30th sept
BT financial breakdown for 29th sept
HB *e-mail plans*
BT plans to be completed by 3rd oct
BT checklist by 30th sept
BT financial breakdown for 29th sept

The quick way to do this is to type 'sort out', 'item list' or similar and press Enter. Use the arrow key to choose No for Timed entry and press Enter. Now press Menu and choose Entry/Edit memo (–+) to go into a blank notepad with your 'sort out' title at the top. This is the memo pad and you've got plenty of space and full wordprocessor facilities to sort out your list, and life – more of which in the next chapter. Choose Exit to leave the memo.

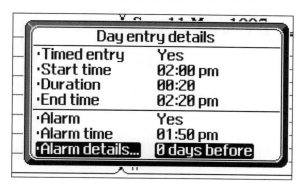

Under today's date at 2pm type 'email team' and press Enter. Fill in the Day entry details as Timed entry No and Alarm Yes. Other entries with alarms can be set for the rest of the afternoon to keep you on your toes.

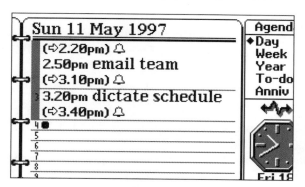

This batch of entries could be entered as To-dos but the quick, alarmed, reminders should do the job and get everything out of the way before you leave on Friday afternoon. You can use Data to bring up contact details to make your phone calls and send your electronic mails.

Now that everyone has been informed and set tasks for the fortnight, you can set an entry to bring up a reminder checklist when you return from holiday. Move forward to a fortnight Monday, move to 9am and type

Catch up reminder

Complete the Day entry details as Timed entry No and Alarm No.

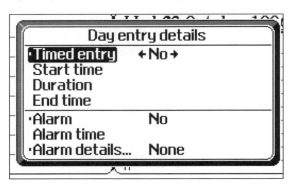

Press Menu and choose Edit/Change entry type (Shift⌒C) and choose To-do. Make this Priority 1, Dated Yes and Alarm Yes. Alarm... is set at 0 days before. Press Tab on Alarm to fill in the details. You are given an alarm of 8.45am, which will jog your memory on the way into work in case you've forgotten your check list. You may be back the Sunday before so you can go over your check list the evening before you return to work by setting the Days previous to 1 and the Alarm at to an appropriate time.

Now press Menu and choose Entry/Edit memo (−+) and type in your checklist to revive the project you're working on. You can copy text from the 'sort out' memo you wrote earlier if this helps. These are probably the items you will have to check when you return.

Birthday

Finally you must place a reminder in the diary to send a card to your mum for her birthday. You can choose to set the reminder a few days before the birthday or you can let Agenda sort it out for you. When you set the reminder on the birthday date. You'll see what I mean . Use the arrow key to move to the diary page of the birthday date. With the arrow key, move the round black cursor to a suitable time for a holiday − 10am will do − and type 'send birthday card to mum' and press Enter.

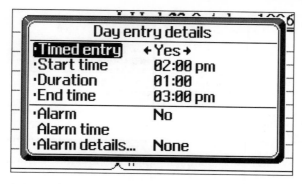

Use the arrow key to choose No for Timed entry, Yes for Alarm and adjust the time to suit – Agenda loves to anticipate your ability to leave things to the last moment and offers 9.00am, but this is not suitable for a holiday morning!

On waking to your Psion Series 3's alarm on this particular day of your well-earned break, you'll notice a text reminder to send a birthday card to mum. It's actually a bit too easy to miss the text reminders given by the Psion Series 3 so you may wish to record an aural reminder which acts as an alarm and reminder of what to do. There's a full example of doing this, and more on sound messages, in the chapter on Record.

When you set an alarm in Agenda, Agenda sends this information – one at a time – to the alarm part of the Time application so all the features of an alarm are available to you from Agenda. For instance you can stop, snooze or clear the alarm entry. Indeed it's important to clear the alarm entry once it's finished because this triggers Agenda to send the next alarm setting it has entered in its diary.

Views

Before we move on to memos and outlining and To-do lists, let's just consider the different views which you can use to display the information you have typed into Agenda.

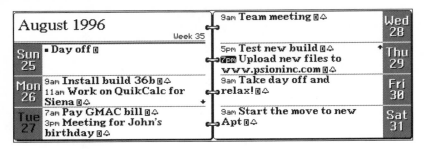

Week view is perhaps the most useful for planning short-term and the working week is, after all, the basic unit of a working person's life.

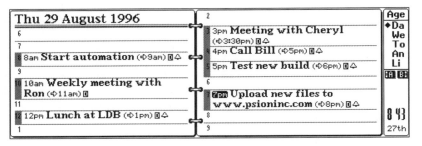

Day view gives you the detail you need in a busy schedule.

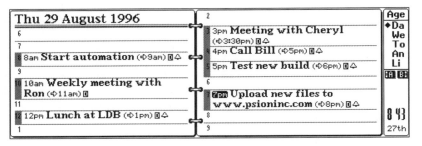

The Year view highlights key days.

&#9823;	**Anniversaries (in 1997)**				Age
	March	April	May	June	Da We Ye To ♦An
	31 michele's birthday (0 years) □» ■	23 annes bday □» ■	4 anthonys bday □» 13 karsten bday □» ■	**12** Mark's bday (0 years) □» ■	
					10 21 16th

Anniversary View lists those never to be forgotten days.

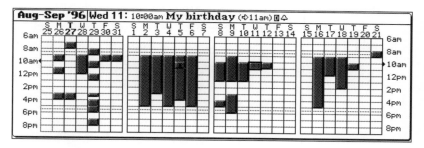

Series 3c owners get a Month view, useful for block bookings – like holidays!

There's More

The role-play we tried out earlier has given you an idea of what Agenda is capable of. In the next two chapters we'll try out more features – with reference to what we've seen so far – and look in detail at all the menu options in the Agenda application.

Chapter 9

Organising and Outlining

 The bit of role-play in the last chapter demonstrated one approach to Agenda. As you try things out you'll find so many options and complete flexibility so that Agenda can encompass your way of working. As we go through the new features in the next two chapters, I'll suggest ways in which the they can be useful.

These chapters can also be used as a reference. Skip bits you don't need at the moment and come back to them to get ideas for their use when you encounter them in daily use. Because of the nature of Agenda I'm jumping around the menu structure quite a bit. Use the menu map appendix or hot-key reference appendix if you are having trouble finding the appropriate menus and their functions.

Remember these points about moving speedily around the menus: within a 'drop down' menu, use the up/down arrow keys to highlight an option. Use the up arrow key to move swiftly from the first entry to the last. In computer jargon it 'wraps round'. Alternatively use the Control key plus the up and down arrow keys to move between the first and last entries. In computer jargon this is 'toggling' between the top and bottom.

Memos

Edit Memo (∪+) is a short key press to a lot of editing. When an entry has a memo attached to it, anything goes because you are launched into a mini wordprocessor.

A memo, in terms of Agenda, is a large note. It might be appropriate to use this feature for a memo about the future; it's certainly the best way to record written information in Agenda if you are using it to keep a diary or to make notes about a meeting. Any entry can be turned into a memo by moving the cursor onto the entry and choosing Entry/Edit memo (∪+). A mini wordprocessor, no less, pops up with your entry note as a title in the centre and with a flashing cursor, also centred, ready for typing. In the right-hand top corner you'll see two ♦ selections in Normal and Outline.

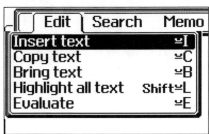

It's worth a quick tour of this mini wordprocessor through its menus. Edit offers the standard Insert, Copy and Bring text. Bring is especially interesting because you can open up Word, the full wordprocessor, to write your memo or make notes in Jotter (Series 3c only) and then copy that text to the clipboard and Bring it into your memo.

Also, if you have an existing memo which contains material you wish to repeat, Copy the text in that memo and return to your new memo to Insert it. The Edit/Highlight all text option is useful for carrying out this Copy and Insert action described above or for applying a Paragraph attribute (Font, Alignment and so on).

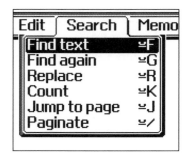

The Search menu has the same trio – Find text, Find again and Replace – as available in the full Word wordprocessor. The Count (in words), Jump to page and Paginate functions prove that the memo editor is capable of multi-page documents so if you keep an extensive diary, for personal reasons, for study or business, you've got all the tools at your disposal here. Which brings us to the Memo menu.

Memo Outlining

Don't let new projects overwhelm you. Take your time and organise your thoughts with the help of the outline feature! Outline is also available in Word so everything you learn here is applicable to that application.

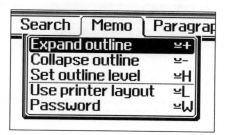

Whether it's a report you've got to compile, an important letter – such as a job application or a sales pitch – or you need to get your thoughts down in a hurry, switch to outline mode.

Since it's so wonderful, let's get using it. But what is an outline? I thought you'd ask so I prepared an outline of what you can use it for

organising ideas

- from thoughts
- from notes
- brainstorming

constructing a document

1. beginning
2. middle
3. end

Do you get the idea? An outline is a structured list which provides a framework for your ideas.Follow the PsiGuide to learn how to get the best out of this superb feature for helping you pull notes together.

Priority Levels

Choose Style/Style gallery (SᴗG) to and use the arrow keys to study the attributes of each style definition. These predefined styles – size, indentation etc – are applied to text to give it a particular look/layout. Note the last field in the style definition, Outline level. This is a priority (the outline level) which is attached to the style, and which determines how text in this style will appear in the outline.

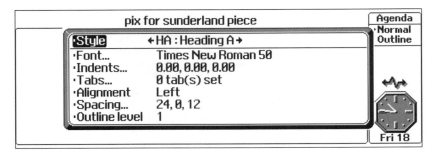

The predefined styles include two headings with a priority of 1 and 2 (the highest available). The body text style has a priority of 9 (the lowest level available). Use the headings styles for your main ideas, the second heading style for your sublist and the body text for fleshing out the ideas. Other styles can be defined or have outline levels given to them so you can create your own set of styles, with priorities 1 to 9, appropriate for outlining. There are full details on editing styles in the chapters on Word.

Once you've typed in the headings, lists and body text, pressing the ◆ key will put you into outline mode, which will display only the range of outline levels which you have specified in Memo/Set outline level (∪H).

In Set outline level you are given 1 as the start number – in other words priority 1 headings are always displayed – and you type in the end number. This gives you plenty of scope for eight subheading style levels and one plain body text style. Depending on what 'overview' of the document you wish to display, or print, you can adjust this outline level.

If you want bullets (blobs at the start of each line in the list) and/or numbers then you have to type these in with the text. The outlining process doesn't put them in automatically.

Because your Psion Series 3 doesn't show all style attributes on screen, you may find it useful to move to Special/Set preferences and to change Show style bar to Yes in the Set Preferences dialogue. A column appears on the left-hand side of your text which indicates, by displaying an abbreviation, which style is currently applied.

PsiGuide begins... Creating an outline

In the Memo editor, press the Control key and, holding it down, press the H and A keys in turn. Now type

send out project info

and press Enter. Press the Control key and, holding it down, press the H and B keys in turn. Now type

e-mail internal project team

and press Enter. Press the Control key and, holding it down, press the B and L keys in turn. Now type

e-mail plans

and press Enter. Press the Control key and, holding it down, press the B and L keys in turn. Now type

e-mail doc

and press Enter. If you wish you can type text after the e-mail plans and e-mail doc items. You will notice that the styles Heading A (HA), Heading B (HB) and Bulleted List (BL) were applied as you typed the codes. The other text has the default style of Body Text (BT).

Press the ◆ key and you'll see the text in outline levels 1 and 2. Other outline levels are not displayed. Call up Memo/Set outline level (^H) and press 3 in the dialogue. Press the ◆ key again to see the outline levels 1 to 3, that is styles HA, HB and BL.

PsiGuide ends

More Menus

Also in the Memo menu is Use printer layout (∪L), which is only useful if you've typed a large memo which you intend to print and which might format in a subtly different way when displayed according to the printer driver.

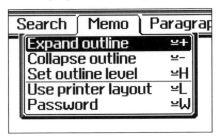

Password protection has its obvious uses in a private diary.

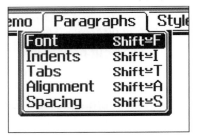

The Paragraph menu is where you adjust the appearance of the words in your memo and is only useful if you are going to print out from here. The Styles plays an important role in outlining but the actual look of the stylescan be ignored if the memo is only ever to be read on screen.

The Special menu contains Set preferences, which determines what type of information you see on screen relating to your document, and the print related options.

Bring Text

We've touched on it, but because of the nature of Agenda at the hub of your personal organising, it's worth reminding ourselves that the Edit/Bring entry (∪B) menu option transfers information from another application into Agenda.

For example, if you're working in Word, you can jot down your aide-memoire, let's say 'remember mum's birthday card' and then later send it to Agenda as an entry in your diary, in this case as a To-do entry. In Word, use the Shift and arrow keys to highlight the aide-memoire and choose Copy text (∪C) in the Edit menu.

Now switch to Agenda and move to the To-do list, use the arrow keys to move to the empty line at the bottom of the list and choose Edit/Bring entry (∪B). Your aide-memoire is now in place. Owners of the Series 3c and Siena can use Jotter in a similar manner.

We'll be making plenty of entries and adding repeats and other properties in the next chapter. We'll also fully investigate the To-do view. There's more to it than first meets the eye.

....

Chapter 10

Agenda Plus

 We'll take on the sharp end of Agenda now as we set ourselves some goals by using the To-do feature to its full extent. You can have multiple To-do lists, crossed out entries, sorted lists, priorities, styles and even repeating To-dos. Better put some time aside for all this. Make it an Agenda entry now!

To-do Details

We finished the last chapter by inserting an entry in the To-do list for a reminder to send a birthday card. Press Enter over this entry and the To-do details dialogue comes up. Use the arrow keys to move to each entry in turn. Don't use Enter because this will close the dialogue box. Type in 1 for priority – it's your *mum's* birthday card after all! Use the right arrow key to change the Dated entry to Yes, from No. The fields below now become active and you can define in more detail this To-do. Use the arrow keys to move to Due date and type in the date.

```
                To-do details
 ·Priority          1
 ·To-do list        projectX
 ·Dated             Yes
 ·Due date          25/11/1996
 ·Date details...   0 days warning
 ·Alarm             No
 ·Alarm details...  None
```

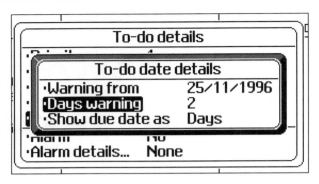

Date details... has its own dialogue so press Tab and type in today's date in the 'Warning from' field. When you move down to the 'Days warning' field, the number of days between today and the day you have to get your mum's card automatically appears. Move to 'Show due date as' and press the right arrow key twice to move from Auto to Days.

projectX	ProjectY
① hire AV equipment ② order stationary ① call conference room ■ remember mums birthday card (30 days)	▪

You'll see the effect of this when you press Enter twice to complete the dialogues. The 'Remember mum's birthday card' entry appears in the To-do list with the number of days remaining in brackets after it.

To edit entry details in the To-do list, arrow key over the entry and press Enter twice – the first press produces a cursor for editing the text message, the second brings up the dialogue. We didn't set an Alarm for our new entry but, using your knowledge of the Alarm application acquired in an earlier chapter, you could easily do so.

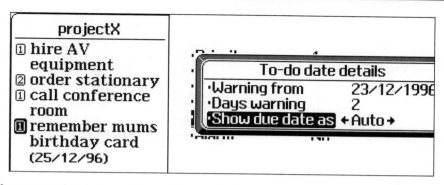

If you use the Auto setting in Due date then the To-do entry appears with a warning in brackets along the lines of (Fri) or (Tomorrow). If you set the Date option then the due date appears in brackets. Each entry can have its own properties so you can choose those appropriate to the job in hand. Remembering a birthday might be done best by date with an alarm set a few days before as a reminder in case you need to post something.

Project Work

A project deadline looming at work might be best dealt with by setting the due date and then counting down the days to go! For large projects create a new To-do list from the To-do list menu – it will appear in the To-do list display by pressing the right arrow key.

If you have a project which contains a number of targets on the way to completion then a good approach is to enter each target with its Due date and Days countdown.

projectX	ProjectY	projectZ	Age
⬚ hire AV equipment ⬚ order stationary ⬚ call conference room ⬚ remember mums birthday card (25/12/96)	▣ target1 (2/12/96) ▣ target2 (4/12/96) ▣ target3 (8/12/96) ◼	▪	Da We Ye ◆To An ◀◆▶ 7:11 25th

Give all the targets the same priority level – make it 9 perhaps – to make sure they are grouped together in your To-do list. You then have a complete picture of the project in stages and entries can be deleted as you hit your targets, or adjusted slightly if you don't.

◀ Bills	To-do
▥ Rent (Thu) ▯	▥ Test QuikCalc for Siena ▯
▥ Phone (Sat) ▯	▥ Upload new graphics for
▥ Elect (Sat) ▯	Series 3c and Siena launch ▯
▥ Cellular bill (9/3/96) ▯	▥ Work on content for new
▥ GMAC (9/9/96) »	site ▯
▥ Car Insurance (9/6/96) ▯	▥ Test FigureIT for Siena ▯
▥ Visa Gold (9/10/96) ▯	▣ Call Ali re the new products ▯
▥ Movers (9/14/96) ▯	▪

Another set of deadlines of a financial nature tend to occur each month. Why not use a separate To-do list to remind you about your outgoings?

Entry Menu

Entry is an Agenda-specific menu with some interesting functions. Firstly Set alarm for entry (⊍L) duplicates the Alarm details available when creating an entry in Agenda, which allows you to update an entry to have an alarm. The dialogue is the same as for the Day entry details/Alarm details dialogue, including an option to choose the alarm sound and to test it.

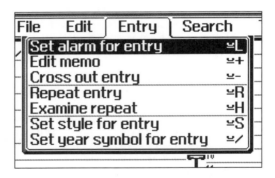

Next in the Entry menu is Cross out entry. Use this to make an entry as no longer valid without actually deleting it. This is very useful when you want to cross a meeting or task off tour agenda but in the knowledge that it might be reinstated. A crossed-out entry literally appears with a line through it.

When the cursor is on a crossed-out entry, the Entry menu changes to show Reinstate entry (⊍-) which you use to vivify the entry. There are lots of potential uses for crossing out, some of which are discussed with To-do lists in this chapter.

The Cross out/Reinstate entry hot key (⊍-) is one of those hot-keys which toggle (turn on and off) a feature in your Psion Series 3.

Agenda doesn't use text styles within its own messages so you have control over the appearance of entries. This can be used to provide another level of urgency or method of labelling certain entries.

Year view contains a lot of information and you can choose to have entries displayed upon it if you wish. Set year symbol for entry is where you choose the character to be used in the year view for a particular entry. By 'coding' certain entries, you can tell from the year view what type of entry is being displayed. For instance, you might choose to use an exclamation mark for particularly important entries.

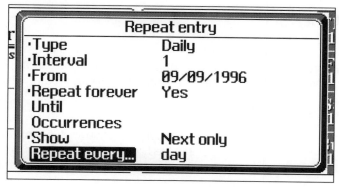

Repeat entry (∪R) offers a dialogue form to fill in. By default the Type field reads No repeat but we are here because we want to repeat the entry so here goes. Use the arrow keys to change to one of the following: Daily, Weekly, Monthly by date, Monthly by days, Yearly.

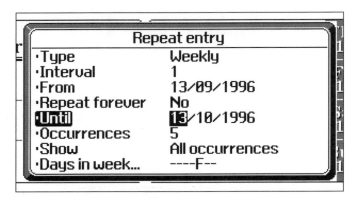

Use the arrow keys to try them out and notice how the details below change to suit. Isn't this useful? In the yearly category you can immediately slot annual reminders such as car tax, house insurances, business year ends, factory holidays and so on.

Monthly entries such as house mortgage, council tax etc can go in. Weekly events, such as planning meetings and Friday night's pub crawl after work can be noted! If you have a daily routine then here's your reminder regime, automatically filled in for you day by day. If your Psion Series 3's memory is taking over from your own brain then you could even have a daily reminder to put out the milk bottles at night!

Repetition

Seriously, the Repeat entry dialogue is a goldmine and you should experiment with it to find out what it can do for you. Here's a brief example to follow through. Get into the Repeat entry dialogue with ↻R. Use the arrow keys to choose Monthly by days, then interval 1 and from today's date, which should be in the From field. Change Repeat forever to No and adjust the Until date below by adding 3 to the month's number.

As you move onto the Occurrences field you'll notice that Agenda calculates how many days in the month are involved. Keep Show All occurrences and press Tab over Days in month... to get the Set days for monthly repeat dialogue. Salaries are often paid on the third Friday of the month or on a specific date (use Monthly by date) so I'm setting this up for Occurrence in month Third, Day in week Friday.

The three buttons in the bottom panel of this dialogue allow you to Set (+) or Clear (-) each of the entries you set up in the top panel. When you have set and cleared to your heart's content, you press Enter to Confirm.

Flexible Repeat

If you set repeat for a day other than the day it's already on then you get two days set. Once you've set an entry as repeating, you'll be offered the chance to edit all the entries globally (all at once) when changing the entry in any way. When you change the repeat details for a repeat entry the Change repeating entry dialogue offers these choices:

Whole entry

This occurrence onwards

Up to this occurrence

This latter item is useful for keeping the main details of an entry – a meeting with someone at some location for instance – but changing the frequency on date/day. In other words, when a holiday intervenes, you can bring your regular meeting forward to get it out of the way before heading for the sun and your normal schedule can resume on your return.

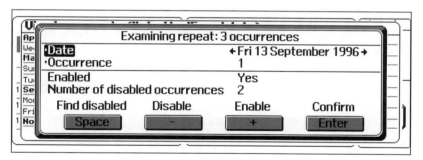

The Examine repeat (∪H) menu option produces the Examining repeat dialogue which helps you keep track of the, potentially numerous, repeat entries you've generated. You need to move the cursor onto a repeat entry before using hot-key ∪H. The arrow keys change the Date field to the dates or days concerned, restricted by the original time constraints placed on the repeat entry.

The Occurrence field just takes you through the entries in numerical order. The bottom panel contains three buttons to Disable (-), Enable (+) and Find disabled (Space). If the entry currently displayed is enabled (Enabled Yes) then pressing - will disable it and pressing + will re-enable it.

This is another way of dropping one or more of the regular repeating entries on of the list, to make way for a bank holiday for instance. Once an entry has been disabled it won't appear in the general Agenda views so the Find disabled button is useful to locate a disabled entry should it need re-enabling. Perhaps someone who couldn't attend your regular weekly meeting, can now do so and it needs re-enabling to remind you that this is now the case.

In the Search menu there's the useful View all repeats (∪V) option, which neatly sums up those entries which keep on coming around. As you can see, the Repeat entry feature is pure gold, at the risk of repeating myself.

Private Investigation

You can quickly amass vast amounts of information in Agenda and some kind of search tool is vital.

The Find dialogue is pretty comprehensive and allow restrictions to be applied when you can remember where an entry may be confined by date or type.

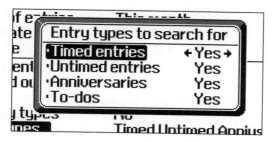

As usual with searches, if you aren't successful then you can widen the search be relaxing the criteria.

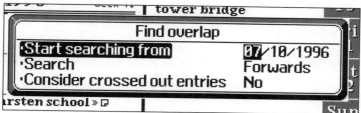

An important management tool for the diary is to check for clashes between different appointments and tasks.

Use Find overlap and restrict your search to the coming few weeks or to a specific period in the future you are worried about. You can search backwards so don't worry if you are not on today's date when applying this.

When you press Enter you'll get a 'scanning' message and, if there is one, the cursor will rest upon the next overlap found. The overlapping time is indicated by a black band. Hitting Enter will take you into the offending entry to change it if required. The Search menu also provides a Calendar display – which is not the Year view. It can be useful to have the conventional layout in front of you.

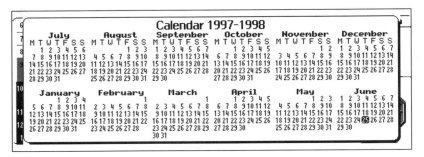

Preferences

The first item under the Special menu is Set preferences (∪Q).

When you select this item a submenu of six views is listed – the same six as controlled with the ♦ key. The view which you are currently in (the one with the ♦ beside it) will be highlighted in the View preferences submenu but you can use the arrow keys to choose any of the six. There are very different dialogues for each view.

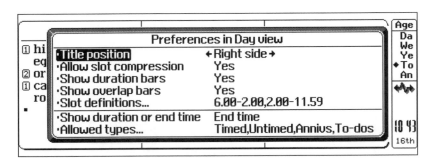

In Day view you can choose left or right side for the Title position. You can turn on and off Slot compression, which means that the lines which separate each hour of the day diary view will either be crunched together (Allow slot compression Yes) when you make entries or the space between the lines will stay the same (Allow slot compression No) and you'll need to scroll with arrow keys to see the rest of the day's hourly slots.

Show duration bars refers to the grey vertical bar which appears beside a timed entry to indicate the length of a meeting or visit etc. I think they perform a function, but you can choose. Show overlap bars are even more useful in my opinion because they serve as a visual reminder when you are packing in timed entries which overlap a little. If you think it's messy, choose No to Show overlap bars.

Time Travel

Slot definitions is a complete dialogue of its own so press the Tab key to get into the form. Here you can define precisely the time limits of your slots and whereabouts on the screen (left or right side) certain slots should appear. For instance, an early riser will probably be happy with the default settings of 06:00am to 02:00pm on the left side of the diary Day view and 02:00pm to 11:00pm on the right side. If very little happens before 09:00am then it might be better to start at 09:00am and finish at 02:00pm on the left side, which gives more space (not more time of course!) for each slot entry.

At the other end of the day - especially if you live in Spain or Italy - 11:00pm is the start of the evening for some people! So, given a Siesta from 02:00pm until 04:00pm, the right side could begin at 04:00pm and end at 11:00pm. Here we have a problem for real night birds since this is a Day view and these settings must stay in bounds.

If you have appointments in the early hours then remember which day it is and adjust the start time appropriately. In some professions (police, manufacturing etc) it is necessary to work a cycle of different shifts so you can use these preferences settings to adjust the 'window' through which Agenda sees your day.

If you want more or less time allocated to each slot then you can change between 5 minutes and 8 hours but anything under 30 minutes gets tiny on screen and a long appointment can be a timed entry so keep slot times sensible.

More Settings

There are two further settings. Show duration or end time is a handy option, and you can choose Neither if you find the slot times easy to use. The duration appears in brackets after the entry eg (1hr) and the end time is shown after the entry in brackets as an arrow pointing to the end time eg (->1pm). The final setting is Allowed types... Use the Tab key to see the four types of entry allowed in Day view, each with a Yes beside it by default. If you want to exclude one of these types then move to the type and use the arrow keys to change to No.

You may wish to exclude the use of Day view for To-do entries if you are trying to keep track of your To-dos through the To-do menu for instance.

Other Views

Week view preferences also provides control over Title position, Show duration or end time and Allowed types...

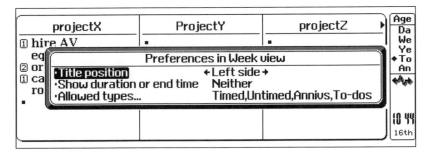

They each operate as described above for Day view.

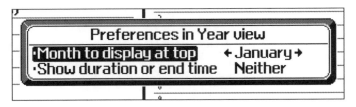

Preferences in Year view also controls Show duration or end time – default neither – and a second option to choose which month to display at the top of the Year view list. January is on top by default but different months begin the year in different countries and religions.

The business year begins in April so this might also be an appropriate choice. Better still, put August at the top of the list and begin the year with a holiday!

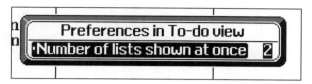

The To-do Preferences dialogue is limited to one setting. The To-do Settings (∪U) contains the real nitty gritty – see later.

If you want more than two To-do lists then you need to be mindful of how the display will turn out, although, by using the arrow keys to scroll up and down and move sideways to other lists, it's surprising how much information you can have side by side. You can only show as many To-do lists as you have active at the time.

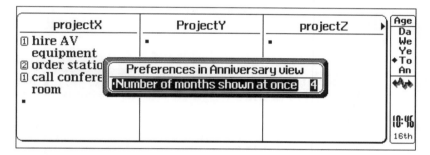

Preferences in Anniversary view controls Number of months show at once (default 2, maximum 4). The more months the merrier for me – I need to build up to some of my anniversaries!

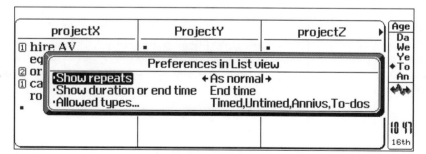

Preferences in List view has two familiar controls over Show duration or end time and Allowed types... which operate as described above under Day view. The new preference is Show repeats which offers As normal (default) and

Once only. I think Once only is best if you've got lots of birthdays etc which will otherwise feature in your important list of things to do, appointments and so on.

Having looked at Set Preferences in the Special menu, there isn't much more to discuss because the rest of the entries are dealt with in specific chapters on using menus and printing. One tip: keep Wrap on because otherwise entries become unintelligible and it becomes difficult to scroll around them.

To-do List in Detail

The To-do list can get a bit 'random' when you've put in a few entries together with their priorities. The priorities group the entries with the priority number 1 at the top but if you've entered lots of priority 1 projects you may wish to choose more suitable settings.

Agenda lists To-dos in order of priority and then date. If the To-do isn't dated then the order can depend on which entry you last edited, which automatically goes to the end of its priority list.

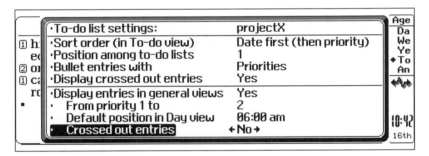

In the To-do lists menu you can choose To-do list settings (∪U) to adjust the list display. Firstly, make sure you are in the correct To-do list, if you have more than one. The Sort order can be changed to Date first so that you can see when your deadlines fall, which is useful to monitor projects by time as opposed to other priorities. There is also a Manual sort option, which activates the Position To-do entry option (Shift∪P).

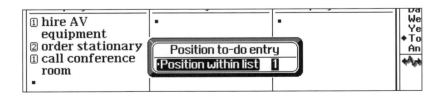

Give this a try. Highlight the first entry in your To-do list and press Shift∪P. A dialogue appears offering to position your entry within the list at position 1. The entry is no longer highlighted so be sure to remember which line you're moving. Just type the number for the position you want to move your entry to and press Enter to get it there.

This is the moment to return to the To-do list settings and the Bullet entries with option. When we moved the To-do entry it would have been easier if the entries had been numbered rather than having priority numbers beside them.

Use the arrow keys to select Numbers as the 'bullets' in front of the To-do entries. Numbering entries can also help organised your list if it has become packed with To-dos with the same priority. Number them and then manually move them into your own priority list.

You can now look at your To-do list from three points of view: by time, by priority (the judgement you put on the task as to its importance) and by your own prioritised (manual) list. All three can be useful depending on the project concerned.

Ordering Your Display

We skipped an entry in the Settings dialogue. If you have created more than one To-do list then you can decide which order you view these. It might be better, for instance, to have your general To-do list displayed first because it will act as a reminder for everyday important jobs.

A special To-do list for a particular project would be second on the list and the preparations for the trip to the Far East you've been promising yourself would be third so you tinker with it from time to time but it wouldn't deflect you from day to day business.

When you cross out an entry in Entry/Cross out entry (∪-) it drops to the bottom of any list and a line is drawn through it. In your setting dialogue you can choose to remove crossed out entries from the display altogether with Display crossed out entries No. The entries will remain crossed out in a sort of cryogenic state and you can thaw them out again by changing this option to

Yes. This effectively gives you three levels of display in normal, crossed out and crossed out not displayed.

You can use this to manage entries which may come and go as projects change their nature, without having to re-enter To-do information. Watch out however when using the File/Tidy option which deletes crossed-out entries!

The bottom half of the settings dialogue effects when happens in the general views rather than the To-do list, that is in the day, week etc views. If you choose Display entries in general views No then end of story: To-dos don't appear. If Yes, you can choose the priorities which will appear. Having just priority one entries will alert you to important tasks without cluttering up your general views.

Default position in Day view normally plonks your To-dos at 6.30am, in the hope that you'll notice them I suppose! It's not a bad idea to adjust this to the end of the day, leaving the working portion of the day free to make other entries. Of course if you have a more active social life than me, you evenings are going to get a bit crowded.

In normal circumstances having crossed out entries on display in your general views might not be sensible but if, for example, you have a To-do list for a particular project and some aspects of the project have been sidelined but are liable to be revived at the last moment, it's nice to keep these potential tasks in mind.

View List

If you wish to restrict the number of views available from the ♦ key then use the Set up list option on the Special menu.

Managing Files

First on the menu list but covered last? You can use Agenda with multiple files but it's best to get to grips with its day to day working before considering this option. Hence files are last in my book.

When an Agenda file is changed, the change is 'saved' automatically so there's no need to save the file at the end of each session or when you Special/Exit. If you want to have more than one diary on the go then you can create new diaries with File/New file (∪N).

However Agenda has many ways built into it to distinguish between different types of entry and you can have multiple To-do lists. Think carefully if Agenda can't achieve what you want before you go to the trouble of creating another files.

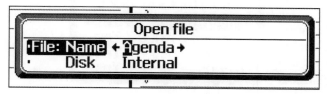

Once you have more than one file, you'll need to open one from within another (File/Open file (∪O).

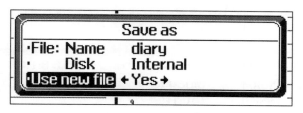

If you want to start a new diary based on information in your current diary, create a 'new' file by using Save as (∪A).

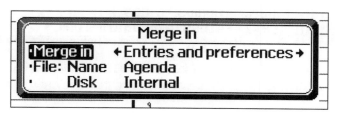

If you do god down the route of multiple diaries then Merge in (∪M) means you can bring two diaries together by merging their files. The Merge in field provides an element of control over the merge. Usually it's a matter of deciding which your 'master' file should be and making sure that all its settings are correct. At this point it's safe to merge entries alone. Running Search/Find next overlap will highlight any clashes caused by the merge.

In the Bin

You can delete Agenda entries from any view so try to get into the habit of getting rid of unwanted and completed entries as you move around the diary. Just highlight the entry and press the Delete key.

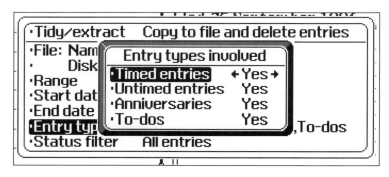

The File/Tidy/extract (⊖T) option provides deletion of entries as a batch. It goes through the diary and removes all your crossed-out entries.

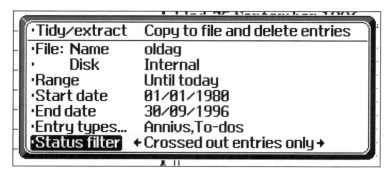

Be careful because I've pointed out that crossing out entries can be used as a means of 'suspending' an entry. If you use Tidy then the entry will disappear completely!

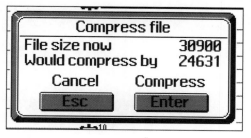

Compress file (⌴K) closes up the gaps in an Agenda file to keep it slim. This is a worthwhile exercise now and again bearing in mind how valuable memory is in your Psion Series 3. For the same reason, keep on deleting!

Chapter 11

Number Time: Psion Calc

Psion Calc is not a pocket calculator equivalent. You'll discover there's more to it than that.

You can use the built-in Calc program to do your number crunching for you, be it for business, study, computer programming, scientific research or engineering. Calculator programs on some desktop computers are very simple affairs, other merely adequate for the sort of office environment in which they are used. The Psion Series 3 calculator differs in that it provides memories, trigonometric functions, powers, logs and other options which we'll go on to discuss below.

Just press the Calc icon on the front of your Psion Series 3 or choose Calc from the System screen to enter the program. What do you see? If this is the first time that you've used Calc then not much. If you've been using it, or someone else has, then the screen will have lines of numbers already on it.

Don't worry, there are only three distinct areas of the screen you need to use Calc. The top line of the screen display shows which memory is in use – M1, M2 etc – and any number stored in that memory. We'll look at memories later. Below are eight lines which are either blank or full of numbers. This area is the 'list' and it contains a record of what has been typed into Calc previously. Below the list is dotted line to keep it apart from the last line which looks like this:

Calc:

There may be some numbers after the colon if Calc is in use and they may be inverted (white on black display). These numbers are the last entry made into Calc and this line is the input line where you type numbers and operators. Finally of course there are menus which you display by pressing the Menu key.

They are Memories, Trig, Powers, Logs and Special and we'll run through them in a moment.

Entering Numbers

The Psion Series 3 Calc also works in a different way from most WIMP-style calculators which merely copy the simplest hand-held equivalents. In the Psion Series 3 Calc you enter numbers, operators (+, -, multiply, divide) and functions into the line at the bottom of the screen. This line can be edited and reworked until you are happy with it. Use the arrow keys to move one character, and Control with the sideways arrow keys to move to the end and beginning of the line.

When entering numbers, use the decimal point as a separator between whole numbers and decimal parts of a number but don't enter a separator for thousands or millions (comma). If you type something in which Calc doesn't recognise or understand then a 'syntax error' message will appear in the bottom right-hand corner of the screen and then the cursor will appear at the point at which the error occurred ready for editing.

The Psion Series 3 Calc understands the four common operators mentioned above, plus < (less than and > (greater than) and % (percentage). The < and > operators produce only two values:

-1   true

0   false

For instance

99<100

gives -1 (true) as a result and

99>100

gives 0 (false) as a result.

The percentage operator is very sophisticated and you can perform a number of useful operations on numbers. Try them out. Type in and press Enter for each of the following to see what results you get.

      10+10%

      10-10%

      10*10%

      10/5%

      100>10%

      100<10%

Calculations List

When you press Enter in the bottom line of Calc the result is displayed and highlighted. The calculation which you typed in pops up to the line above and remains in view. Instead of Enter you can press the = key but it's a difficult key press (Shift +) to achieve.

Press Enter again and the result pops up a line and the calculation appears again in the bottom line. They haven't swapped places but rather everything has moved up one line and the calculation has been redisplayed so that you can edit it if required. To get rid of it just press Delete.

The list always holds the previous calculations carried out in the bottom line. How many of these calculations you can view depends on the Zoom view of the screen you are working in. If you want to see more of the list then go to the Special menu and choose Zoom out (Shift⌣Z) until you've got 13 lines in view. When you next press Enter, the top (first) line disappears to make way for the fourteenth, the second makes way for the fifteenth and so on. Zooming in and out to change character size changes the number of lines in view between six and 13.

Keep Going

While the result is still highlighted you can make use of it in a further calculation either by typing in another operator or by choosing a function from a menu. When you do this it tells the calculator to hold on to the result and re-use it to produce a new result.

If you want to start afresh then type your number and the old result will pop up onto the line above (the bottom line of the list) and your new number will appear in the bottom editable line. If the new number is a negative number press Esc or Delete first to remove the old result to avoid any confusion.

The calculations (and results) which Calc lists are not just a visual record of what's gone before. Rather it's a 'live' list. You can retrieve a value or calculation by using the arrow keys to highlight the information you want to put into the bottom line.

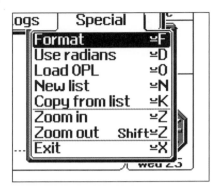

The key combination ⊍Enter or the Special/Copy from list menu option (⊍K) copies the highlighted text into the bottom line, replacing a highlighted result or inserting itself at the cursor if you're in the middle of editing a calculation. You can operate on an item in the list with a menu function before copying it to the bottom line if you wish. If the information in the list is redundant and you want to start afresh, use the Special/New list menu option (⊍N).

Memories

The list of previous calculations remembers what you've typed and the results but there is a different type of memory commonly found on more advanced calculators and, naturally, in your Psion Series 3 Calc.

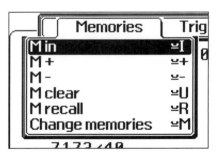

There are ten memories M0 to M9 and the contents of the current working memory (the one which is available at the moment) is displayed at the top of the Calc screen. For instance:

$$M1 = 24$$

```
┌──────────────────────────────────────────┐
│      Change memories                       │
│·List of memories        M2                 │
│·New memory name         M2                 │
│█New memory value█       .750               │
│·Current working memory  M1                 │
└──────────────────────────────────────────┘
32500
```

To view another memory, choose the Memories/Change memories menu option (∪M). You fill an empty memory with the 'M in' menu option (∪I) which takes a value from a result in the bottom line or from a highlighted item in the list. Type your calculation or just a number into the bottom line and press Enter. The result is highlighted.

Now choose Min (∪I) and the value is shown at the top of the screen in the working memory. The M+ and M- operations then add and detract from the value in the current working memory and you can start afresh with M clear (∪U)

Memories retain their values even if you choose Special/Exit and leave Calc so they are handy places to store results or formulae that you want to hang onto for next time.

In Calculations

You can use memories in calculations on the bottom line (how appropriate 'bottom line' is when I'm calculating my incomings and outgoings with Calc!). However M0 doesn't mean much and it pays to assign new names to memories which hold values you are using in a calculation or which will hold the result. For instance M0 can hold .5 and you can use the Memories/Change memories dialogue box (∪M) to choose the memory name and then highlight New memory name, typing 'discount' for the new name and .5 for New memory value if necessary. You can then type:

10*discount

and press Enter to produce

5

Note that you can't hold a formula in a memory, it's the result which goes in. If you want to use a formula over again in the bottom line, it's perhaps easier to drop it down from the list as described above. You can't use a memory value, say 17.5, in a memory called VAT, in a percentage calculation like this:

10<VAT%

It gives an 'unexpected name' or 'name too long' error.

Number Formats

Let's have a quick look at the Special menu and first up is Format (∪F). This dialogue box is where you choose from General, Hexadecimal, Fixed and Scientific formats.

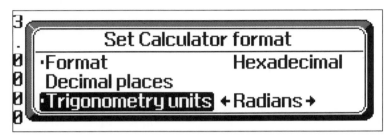

General

General format shows a number with decimal places, up to the limit of 12 digits. When Calc runs out of digits to display a very small or very large number, it converts the number into an exponential number. In this format the number is displayed followed by an 'e' and a second number. The 'e' means 'times ten to the power of' the following number. It moves the decimal place in the first number to the right by the number of places specified in the second number. Therefore 1.2345e4 is the equivalent of 12345.0000.

If you want to enter exponentials into the bottom line of Calc you can do so in the format above. The number contains no spaces. In results, exponentials use a capital E with the + sign after it followed by the second number. If the number really does get out of hand in terms of size you'll get an overflow, underflow or bad number error message.

Hexadecimal

Hex (base 16) is the number base appropriate to computer software and often preferred by computer programmers who need to work 'in sync' with the way the computer does things rather than the way humans do things. A handy feature for Calc to have then for the programming community. A hex number can be entered in any calculation by prefixing it with the & sign. These are the hex numbers with their equivalent decimal:

&1 ,&2 ,&3 ,&4 ,&5 ,&6 ,&7 ,&8 ,&9 ,&A ,&B ,&C ,&D ,&E ,&F ,&10

1, 2, 3, 4, 5, 6, 7, 8, 9, 10,11,12,13,14,15,16

The result of a calculation containing a hex number will be in the current format, usually General i.e. decimal, so:

&A*10=100

If you turn on hexadecimal format:

&A*10=&64

Note that in hexadecimal format you can still enter a decimal. It's the result that's shown in hex. Hex number results are always given to the nearest whole number.

Fixed

The Fixed format works to 12 digit precision as per the General format but the result is rounded to produce a number which conforms to the number of decimal places you specify in the Fixed format. This is useful when 'silly' numbers are unacceptable, for example in an invoice when a 30% discount is levied. You might get:

23.45*82%=19.229

under General format. Use Fixed format to two decimal places and you'll get:

23.45*82%=19.23

which is usable when working in £ and pence, $ and cents, DM and pfennigs etc.

Scientific

Scientific format – sometimes called Standard Form – assumes you're going to work in exponentials as described above. You can specify the number of significant digits and, while accurate to 12 digits, the result will be displayed to the number of significant digits specified. Some scientific equipment may only measure to a certain precision, or accuracy beyond a point may be unnecessary.

This format is useful for very large and very small numbers.

500000000000000

can be written as

5*100000000000000

and

5x*10 14

A number such as

5432100

is the same as

5.432100*1000000

which equals

5.4321x*10 6

The number is between 1 and 10 and it's multiplied by a power of ten. In Calc this becomes

5.43200000000E+06

Very small numbers can also be expressed in scientific notation.

0.00075

equals

7.5x*1/10000

equals

7.5x*10 -4

The power of ten is negative. In Calc the number is shown with the default number of significant digits (12) followed by an E and then the exponent. Thus

0.00075

becomes

7.50000000000xE-04

Use Calc to experiment with exponentials. Entering numbers in this style is covered above under General.

Powers

An Indian philosopher once helped his king and was offered any reward. He asked for one grain of rice on the first square of a chessboard, two grains on the second square, four on the third square, eight on the fourth square, and so on, each doubling the previous number. The king thought he'd got off lightly but he didn't have a Psion Series 3! Multiplying by two by two a total of 63 times (2^63) gives you a lot of rice.

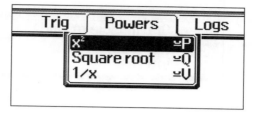

The Powers square function is useful for calculating volume. Just type the value into the brackets which appear in the input line and press Enter.

Trig Functions

Trigonometry means measuring triangles and the three ratios sine, cosine and tangent enable people to work out distances and angles which often can't be physically measured.

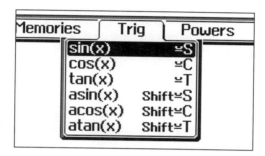

Choose Trig/sin(x) (∪S), enter a number at the cursor inside the brackets and press Enter to get the sine of the number. Choose Trig/asin(x) (Shift∪S) and press Enter and you'll get the number you started with. The asin function automatically works on the number you left highlighted in the bottom line.

Routines

The trig functions we've briefly looked at are, technically speaking, not part of the Calc program. When you select a function from a menu and it's activated by pressing Enter, the calculation is carried out by a 'routine' in the built-in computer language which comes with your Psion Series 3. The language is called OPL an it contains the ability to apply these functions to numbers and so Calc makes use of it. The 'routine' is a mini program in the computer's own machine language. OPL uses these routines by sending a number and receiving a number in return. Don't use CALL, OS, USR.

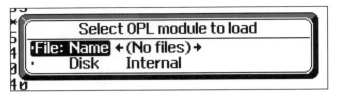

Additional functions to those which come as standard in OPL can be programmed and made available to the calculator's bottom line.

This is beyond the scope of this introduction but it shows the superior flexibility of Calc and is an area you may wish to explore in the future. For more on calculations and number-crunching with your Psion Series 3, don't forget the chapter on Sheet.

Series 3c Calc

Calc on your Series 3c has two modes: Desk and Adv(anced). Desk mode is for everyday calculations where a running total is kept in the bottom window and a 'ribbon' display of the ongoing elements of the calculation on a 'readout' at the top. Desk's operation is that of the familiar desktop office calculator. The Advanced mode operates as described at the beginning of this chapter. All the functions described in this chapter are of course available.

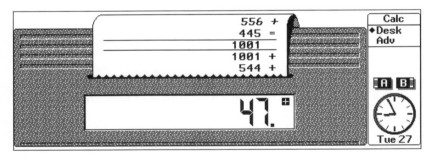

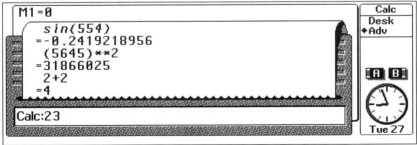

Alternative Calc

Look out for Calc3a, possibly the ultimate Shareware calculator for the Psion Series 3. It offers about 60 mathematical functions, a database feature for your equations and conversion formulae, graphical X-Y plots and statistical calculations with up to 1000 data points. Each function is assigned to one of the keys. The $10 registration fee gets you a 30 page manual. See the Appendix on Shareware for further information about applications other than those available as standard in your Psion Series 3.

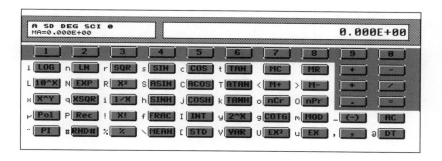

Chapter 12

Psion Word

Working with words is not easy on a small keyboard but but this book was written mainly on a Psion Series 3! Read on and learn how to get great documents from your Psion Series 3's wordprocessor.

Wordprocessing is what we do most on desktop computers. On the Psion Series 3 the keyboard is a barrier to producing large documents. However notes, letters and brief business documents such as reports, can be produced without pain. Word contains sophisticated wordprocessing tools to make your life easier so reading this chapter will pay back in time saved at the keyboard.

Series 3c owners should remember that they can use their Jotter application to make short notes and then transfer them into Word to contribute to larger documents. Information from other applications, such as names and addresses from Data, can also usefully be transferred into Word.

Writing to your MP has never been easier. The spreadsheet is a less well-understood tool but is becoming equally significant, linking its numerical data with graphics presentation software so that the less numerate can also understand what's going on. I'll take a look at these main applications in detail over the next few chapters, beginning here with the wordprocessor.

Versatile

More than any other application software, the wordprocessor has to be the most versatile of programs. On the Psion Series 3 a wordprocessor can be expected to perform the main tasks of editing text but also to spell check it (Series 3a 1Mb and above), and produce an attractive layout on an available printer.

Wordprocessing means different things to different people. You could use a wordprocessor for preparing an essay or article which needs to have page numbering and the same heading on all the pages. You could prepare a letter to customers telling them about a new product, ready for personalising by mail merging the letter with individual names and addresses from a database. You could be inspired to produce the twenty carefully devised words to create an effective advert for your next rave!

Documents

Wordprocessor files are often referred to as documents and this word can apply to both the document you are displaying in Word and to Word files which have been saved.

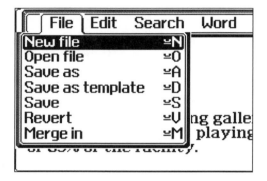

Word's File menu contains the usual options for a Psion application, plus two specifics in Save as template and Merge in, both of which are covered later in this chapter.

Moving Around

In the same way it's worth learning as many hot-keys as you can, it's also worth remembering that you can use the Control and ∪ keys in combination with the arrow keys to move the text cursor around a document. The text cursor is the blinking vertical line which tells you where the next keyboard character is going to go. By moving the cursor to the middle of a word you can insert a character. A reminder of the keyboard layout is shown opposite.

If you don't have a document to work with, type in a few words at random on different lines and try out the Control and Psion combinations with the arrow keys to get a feel for moving to the end of a word, start and end of line and to top and bottom of the document.

Action	Keypress
Delete character to left of cursor	Delete
Delete character to right of cursor	Shift Delete
Move one screenful	∪ up/down arrow keys
Move top/bottom	Control ∪ up/down arrow keys
Highlight next character	Shift left/right arrow keys
Highlight next line	Shift up/down arrow keys
Highlight current word	Control Shift ∪ left arrow key
Highlight current paragraph	Control Shift ∪ right arrow key
Delete to the beginning of line	∪ Delete
Delete to the end of line	Shift ∪ Delete

Table 11.1. Shortcuts cut down on key presses.

Playing with Text

Using a wordprocessor can be great fun. Whatever the standard of your typing, you can always get it right eventually! Just keep typing. There's no need to press Enter at the end of lines because something called 'word wrap' takes care of it automatically. Press Enter when you want to start a new paragraph. Place the cursor at the start of a paragraph and press the Delete key to bring two paragraphs back together.

You can edit your text by selecting it and choosing to delete it, move it elsewhere in the document or copy it. Press the Word icon and type in a bit of Robert Louis Stevenson

> **Dark brown is the river,**
>
> **With trees on either hand.**
>
> **It flows along for ever,**
>
> **Golden is the sand.**

But I've got it wrong. Lines two and four need to be swapped around. It's time to use the Shift key in combination with the arrow keys. Position the text cursor at the beginning of line four. Hold down Shift key and press the right arrow key. The cursor moves to the right and highlights the text as it goes. If you press for too long, the cursor drops down onto the next line. If this happens, press the left arrow key to retreat back to the end of line four. When the whole of line four is highlighted, press Delete. No, I haven't gone mad. Delete keeps a copy of the deleted text in something called the clipboard. The clipboard is an area of the Psion 3a's memory which has been put aside to keep the last chunk of deleted or copied text.

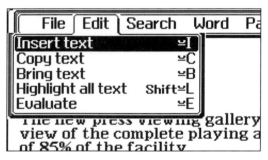

Now move the cursor up to the start of line two, press Menu and press Enter over Edit/Insert text (∪I). You now have the copy of line four at line two. Line two is now line three but should be line four! Repeat the process above for the new line three and copy it to the last line. If you get it right you will have swapped lines two and four in the verse above.

Word also has a Copy text function which copies the highlighted text but doesn't delete it. To demonstrate the difference between what you've just done and using Copy text, highlight line four of the verse again. Menu and press Enter over Edit/Copy text (∪C). Move the cursor to line two and press ∪I. You now have line four, still highlighted, on line two and line two immediately following. Press Enter again to move the second line down one line. You've copied the fourth line to the second but now you have a fifth line you don't need!

Clean Copy

Copy is not very useful in the above scenario. It's very useful when you have a repetitious list to produce. For instance, a price list. Type in the basic phrase 'Baked Beans – pack of ? – price £?.??'. Highlight the phrase, press ∪C and press Enter and ∪I in turn as many times as you need the phrase. Then move down the lines of text adjusting the first ? to the pack quantity and the £?.?? to the price. You can even use Search and Replace to change this ?s if you wish – see searching and replacing later.

Analyse any piece of work you are producing to see what repetition is involved and then use Copy and Insert to your advantage.

Moving text is usually known as 'cut and paste'. However in Word there's no cut command so it's more 'delete and paste'. The delete or copy action stores the text out of sight temporarily until you position the cursor where you want the text to go and paste it in (Insert). The terms come from the design industry where, before computers, the artist would use a knife to cut out the paper with the text on and glue it into position somewhere else.

Magic Spell

Because the Psion Series 3 keyboard is difficult to use, a technique you may like to try is what I call 'kamikaze typing'. It's not as drastic as it first sounds! In the vernacular, it means 'go for it'. Type as fast as you can without worrying about mistakes you know you are making. Try to hit the space bar at the right moments but don't worry about anything else. When you've finished use the spell-checker to tidy it up.

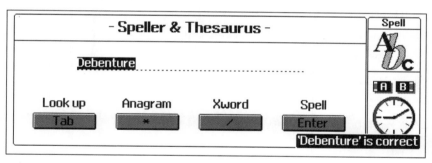

The spellchecker (∪∪) is a program which works together with a couple of dictionaries which are held on disk. It's pretty stupid really and only knows words which are in these dictionaries. Therefore the bigger the dictionary, generally the better at spelling it is. Each word in your document is checked to see if it is identical to a dictionary entry. If the word is not found, you are informed and you can change it if it is obviously wrong, choose one of the words which the checker will suggest for you (Accept), or you can 'teach' the spellchecker the word because it is correct but not in the dictionary (Add).

The spell-checker will pick up your typing errors as mis-spelled words and will guess what you mean't to type. Many of the words will be quickly corrected in this way. A final visual check and some manual editing will get your document into shape. Often this kamikaze method is quicker than trying to correct every mistake as you make it. Try it out and see if it suits your style.

You can use the Thesaurus (∪T) in a slightly more creative fashion by looking for synonyms (alternative words of a similar meaning) so that you can vary the vocabulary in your document. This is more useful for creative, rather than business or technical, writing. It's one of the ways in which you may develop a style of writing, whether it's for letters to friends, or for a novel.

Search and Replace

Search and replace is another useful standard tool on a wordprocessor. For instance I've just written this piece using 'wp' to denote wordprocessor, that's two characters I had to type every time I wanted wordprocessor in my text, not 13. I've then chosen to search for 'wp' and to replace it with 'wordprocessor' and I chose to do so selectively so that I could keep the 'wp's above.

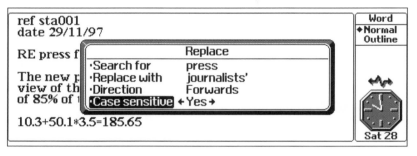

Choose Search/Replace (∪R), type

wp

into the Search for field and

wordprocessor

into the Replace with field. Word checks forwards or backwards so move to the start of a document first and choose Direction Forwards if you want to check the whole document.

Case sensitive should usually be Yes. When you've completed the Replace dialogue box, press Enter. When the first 'wp' is found, Word pops up a dialogue at the bottom of the screen

(E)End   (R)Replace   (S)Skip   (A)All

End just stops the process, R replaces 'wp' with wordprocessor, S skips this 'wp' and finds the next (selective replacing), and A replaces all the 'wp's with wordprocessor in the remainder of the document (non-selective replacing).

PsiGuide begins... Searching for text

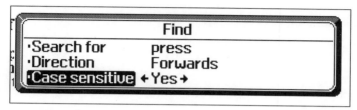

If you want to find a piece of text in your Word document, or you've left a marker then use Search/Find text to locate it. Press ^F and type in the text 'string' you are looking for. 'String' is a computer term for a sequence of alphabetic or numeric characters.

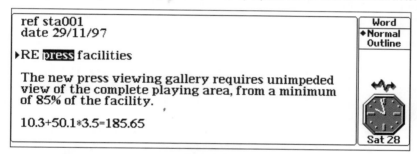

When the required text is found, it is highlighted and displayed in position. At this point you can choose to make a change. Note that the word is highlighted ready to be replaced by your typing. If you wish to edit something else, use the arrow keys to move to the correct spot.

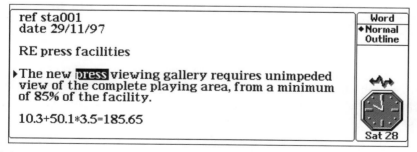

If this isn't the instance of the text you want to find then immediately press ^G to find the next appearance of the text in your document.

PsiGuide ends

Clever Merging

Word can't perform what's known as 'mail merging' but it can achieve the same results pretty easily. For instance Search and replace can be used to generate individual versions of a form letter. For instance you can write one letter to send to all your relations at Christmas. At the top of the letter you type

Dear Relation

Before you print each letter, you can search and replace the 'Relation' with the real name, thus creating an individual letter.

Another method of doing this is to use the Edit/Bring text (∪B) option. Press the Data icon to go into Data. If you don't already have any records entered then create something to experiment with now. If you are in find mode, press the key to move into data entry mode. The cursor is positioned after the Name: field so type in a name, press Enter four times to move to the Address: field and type in a brief address. Use the Shift and arrow keys technique to highlight the full text of the card and choose Edit/Copy text (∪C).

Press the Word icon to get back into Word. Position the cursor at the head of the document and choose Edit/Bring text (∪B) to insert the text from Data at the cursor position. Delete the line spaces and you have your address ready at the start of your letter. In this way Bring text can be used to bring in name and address details, email addresses, and spreadsheet figures to enhance your reports.

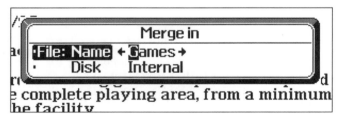

The Merge in (∪M) option on the File menu brings a piece of text into the document on screen at the point you've positioned your cursor but, unlike, Bring text, it drops in an existing file. This then is another way of managing standard letters. You can have some standard paragraphs – chasing new business, demanding money, golf on Friday – saved as documents ready for merging into your current letter.

The Merge in dialogue pops up to help you choose the file by using the left and right arrow keys.

Cutting Keystrokes

Recall for a moment the amount of clicking of the keyboard which you carry out in a typical week of work with your Psion Series 3. Then multiply this by 52 weeks of the year and begin to twig that if you could cut out some of the typing, you could be even more productive. Your Word wordprocessor has some features which can help you in this aim.

Shortcuts

A lot of the key pressing you do may not result in anything typed! When moving around a document – as new ideas come to mind or errors appear – try to use the shortcuts. The movement hot-keys are listed at the beginning of this chapter.

A handy hint when working on a large document is to use a tag of some kind to mark a spot you haven't quite finished or need to refer to. Come up with your own impossible to replicate character combination – @£ for instance – and search for it later. You can also make use of Jump to page (∪J) to move to a distant spot in your document.

Templates/Forms

You can use Word to create standard documents which you can use over and over again to fulfill basic correspondence and communication. Don't imagine you've just got a typewriter equivalent in your Psion Series 3 and that you have to keep writing the same old words over again.

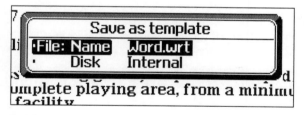

The first stage of a standard letter is the standard text, the details which won't change such as your name and address details. The next layer of information such as date, the way you address the person you're writing to, the signing off – faithfully/sincerely etc – can be kept in one or two sensible combinations by saving (∪D) the letters under different template names such as Standard1 and Standard2 or StanSincere, StandFaith.

```
┌─────────────────────────────────────────┐
│              Create new file              │
│ ·File: Name         project               │
│ ·      Disk         Internal              │
│ ▐Use template▌     ◆Yes◆                  │
│ ·Template: Name     Ants.wrt              │
│ ·           Disk    Internal              │
└─────────────────────────────────────────┘
       the facility.
```

When you create a New file (◡N), arrow key down to the Use template field and change it to Yes. Choose the name of your previously saved template file and, hey presto, you've got the beginning of your new document already sorted out. The template files don't appear on the System screen.

Ready-made Paragraphs

Another use for a template is to store some standard paragraphs of often-required text. Type in your standard paragraphs at the bottom of the document which you save as a template. Create a new file using the template and then copy the standard paragraphs into place as neccessary. Those paragraphs you don't need can be deleted and the standard paragraphs reworked if anything new is required.

Make your paragraphs up from the same number of lines so that printing is not effected or do a quick page preview before printing.

Outlining

You can bash in your words or you can go for a more structured approach through using the Outline feature.

Psion Word uses lists and styles to help clarify the information you enter and create a hierarchy and structure. The, previous, chapter about outlining in Agenda will give you the detail on outlining and some ideas to put into practise. Here we'll quickly recap. Outlining begins with the definition of styles in the Styles/Style gallery and Style housekeeping menus. Each style definition, new or predefined, has an outline level attached to it. This level can be changed as you wish.

As you type your main ideas, apply styles with low outline level numbers, starting with 1. Add to the list with further subheadings with outline levels from 2 to 8 and flesh out the ideas with a body text style with an outline level of 9.

When you press the ◆ key (or ◡+ to Expand outline, ◡- to Collapse outline) to choose between Outline and Normal, the headings, subheadings and sub-

subheadings etc will be displayed according to their outline level priority. The outliner will thus displays the structure of your list to indicate the main points and the secondary points. When in outline mode, the outline can also be printed out.

Layout

As well as the words themselves, a wordprocessor also handles the layout of your document. Presentation these days is very important and Word takes care of the text size, line spacing, paragraph indents and styles such as bold and italic. You can also set the justification of the text, which effects its appearance and readability.

Word also handles the setting up of a document so that the printed version is correctly positioned and looks the part. This is especially useful for checking page breaks. We are about to move on to subjects new but we'll return to Word and the topic of style, layout and printing in Chapters 18 and 19.

Chapter 13

....

Psion
Data

 The Psion Series 3 database is your address, telephone and contact book and much more. Press the Data icon and you can quickly look up information you've previously filed in record cards. You can transfer an existing contacts list from your desktop PC or you can type in details from your paper-based address book.

Data is especially good at keeping track of single 'cards' of information. Each card or 'record' as it's called in a database, can contain a screenful of text. The text can be split up into sections under separate headings. Each section is called a 'field' and each heading is the 'field name'. If you've used databases on desktop computers then you may recognise Database as being of the 'card index' type.

Keeping Track

If you get a call from a business colleague and need to keep his or her details to make contact at a later date then you can quickly capture the information in the database. Press the ON button and the Data button and you're in Data.

The ♦ key switches between the different modes of Data, Find and Add to begin with but you can add Change to this list – indicated by the display in the top right-hand corner of the screen. Since we need to enter details into a blank database record, press the ♦ key so that it rests beside Add.

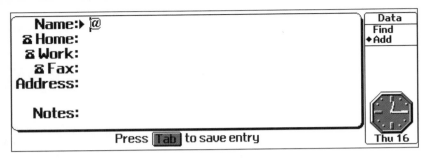

A record display contains lines for Name, telephone Home, telephone Work, Fax, Address and Notes. Each line (or *field* in the database jargon) is a blank area into which you type your information. Type the name and press the down arrow key twice to take the cursor to the Work (telephone) line. Don't use the Enter key to move around the record. Type the number. Add fax and address details if necessary.

These days you'll probably have a mobile telephone number and an e-mail address to note so you may wish to place these on the first two lines of the Notes field. There's a neater way of doing this which we'll look at below – Right Field/Record Design. For now, press the Tab key to save the record.

Saving Times Two

I'd just like to clarify what saving this record involves. Before you press Tab, the information you have typed is on your screen but it's not been accepted into the database. For the record to join the others in the database you press Tab. The database is a sequence of information items held in the memory of the Psion Series 3.

The database, made up of this collection of records which you've saved using Tab, should also be stored as a 'file' on the internal 'disk'. If you press ∪S, the new information is saved into the file called Data by default.

So there are two save processes, one to add the record information you type in to the database (Tab) and one to save the file

You can also press Menu and choose Save as (∪A). Enter the name under which you wish to give the database file, Contacts for example. Note that the internal disk is selected as the place for the file to be saved. In fact Data will choose a place of its own in the internal disk in which to save the file Contacts. There's more information about filling later in the book.

PsiGuide begins... Saving a Data file under a new name

If you've got your Psion Series 3 to hand, try it now.

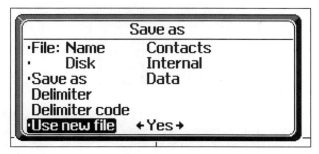

Give your database file as meaningful a name as you can in the eight characters available – try 'Contacts' or for the purpose of our example. Move down to the Use new file field and change it to Yes.

Press the System button to exit the database and you'll see the Data icon on the screen with the name of your file, Contacts, in bold beneath the icon and at the top of the file list. This name is highlighted so if you press the Data icon or Enter you'll go straight into your Contacts database.

If you wish to create a brand new empty file then go into an existing file and then press ∪N and type in a new filename.

PsiGuide ends

Editing a Record

What you put into a record form may turn out not to be what you wanted. It may contain typing errors, the information it contains may change – for instance when British Telecom next change all the telephone code numbers. No problem. Just go to the record to edit. You can do this by choosing Search/Jump to Entry (⌐J).

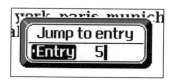

Each record has a number attached to it which is displayed in the bottom right hand corner. It's the first number before the / character. The second number represents the line your cursor is on in the record display. Alternatively you can use Find as described below.

Once you have found the record to edit, press Menu and in the ◆ menu, choose Change (Shift⌐C). The ◆ menu is at the far right-hand side but you can get to it from the File menu by pressing the left-facing arrow key once.

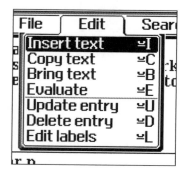

Edit/Update entry (⌐U). gets you to the same place. The standard field names are displayed and you can freely edit and add information. Use the arrow keys to move around rather than press Enter because Enter adds a line and this can disrupt the existing format of the record card.

You can type information into the record 'card' as you did when you first filled it in. When deleting existing text, the delete key quickly removes characters to the left of it but be careful. If you hold the delete key down it will delete characters on the line you start with and then pop up to the previous line and delete there too, which you may not intend.

Like other Psion applications, Data can be configured for your personal use. If you want to have the Change function permanently available through pressing the ♦ key then use the Set up ♦ list option to 'make it so'.

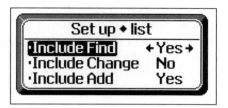

Searching Your Records

We've used Data in Add and Change mode so far. The other mode of operation is Find. Note that these terms are displayed one above the other in the top right-hand corner of the Data screen. Above this list is the file name 'Contacts' which you've given your database.

When you go back into the database and the last thing you did was to save your record (Tab), then you'll be presented with another blank record form ready to add more information. Otherwise you'll find yourself in Find mode and you can tell this because the word Find: appears in the bottom left-hand corner of the display.

Why not check that the previous record information you entered is still there. If you are still in Add mode then pressing the♦ key to go to Find mode. Now type into the Find box which appears at the bottom left of the screen. Type in something you guess is in the record – part of a person's name is usually what you can remember – and press Enter. The record containing the name will appear in front of your eyes. Of course there may be more than one record in the database which contains the combination of letters you have typed in.

```
  Name:▸Mr P Siena
 ☎Home: 01987 654321
  ☎Fax: 456789
Address: london, new york, paris, munich
  Notes: top of the palmtops




 Find: mr p
```

For example if you type 'North' into the Find box you may find an entry for David North, which is what you wanted, but you may also be confronted with a record for Barclays Bank with an address in 'North'ampton. Incidentally Find could equally come up with Barclays in Bridge'n'orth because Find doesn't distinguish between a lower case 'n' and an upper case 'N'.

When you are confronted with a record which you don't want then just press Enter to move to the next which contains some matching information. If no matching record is found then 'Not found' comes up in the centre of your screen.

If you type nothing into the Find box but just press Enter then it will display the first record and you can move to the next with Enter. <Shift Enter> moves to the previous record.

Right Field

I mentioned above that the record layout which your Psion Series 3 database pops up first time is not necessarily appropriate to the kind of information you wish to enter. You can put any information in you like of course but the labels (the titles such as Name, Address etc) are not going to match what you need. I observed that even in a contact database, lines (fields) for e-mail addresses and mobile telephone numbers may be needed. If you are collecting information for a business or school project then the labels could be almost anything at all.

To change the labels in the record 'card', Press Menu and choose Edit/Edit labels (∪L). The card layout appears and the cursor is now active in the area where the bold text labels are placed. You can type very long labels but of course that limits the amount of information which will be in view so a compromise is required.

You can highlight text by pressing <Control><Shift> and moving the arrow keys. This text can then be copied (∪C) and inserted (∪I) elsewhere in the record labels area. This is a handy way of copying the little telephone symbol into other lines.

The symbol isn't just for fun but denotes a line which will be 'broadcast' via the sound system when you choose to automatically 'dial' by pressing ∪Help. Sufficient to say for now that these telephone lines (I) should contain telephone numbers in the correct format if you want them to be automatically dialled. The format is <area code><space><number>. A <-> hyphen character can be used instead of space as a separator if you wish.

When you have finished amending the labels you save by pressing Tab in time-honoured fashion. We are such experienced Psion Series 3 users already! Of course the best time to edit labels is when you first setup the database, more of which below.

PsiGuide begins... Editing labels

Name:
☎ **Home:**
☎ **Work:**
▸☎ **Fax:**
Address:

Choose Edit/Edit labels (∪L) to get the blank 'form' for your data.

Highlight an existing label using the Shift and arrow keys in combination.

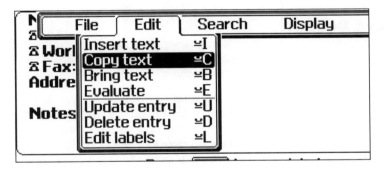

Copy the highlighted text and insert it in the following couple of lines.

Name:
☎ **Home:**
☎ **Work:**
☎ **Fax:**
☎ **Mobile:**
▸☎ **Email:**
Address:

Use the cursor keys and delete key to edit the new fields and type in the new labels
(Mobile, Email) required.

```
   Name:▸Mr P Siena
 ☎Home: 01987 654321
   ☎Fax: 456789
 ☎Mobile: london, new york, paris, munich
 Address: top of the palmtops




 Find: mr p
```

Watch out! If you've already got data typed in then the new labels will not match up with the data in each field.

PsiGuide ends

Record Design

When you create a database the first thing you should do is to design the record layout. Sketch out on paper what information you need, in which order and how many lines each item is likely to require.

Although the screen displays only 12 lines down and 36 across, each record can contain over 4,000 characters. You can keep on typing at the right-hand edge of a record line but if you want to get more of the information in view at the same time then the restriction is a maximum of just 35 characters across because when the cursor which inserts characters reaches the 36th column, the words wrap onto the next line.

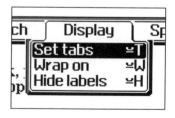

This feature can be turned on and off from the Display/Wrap on menu (◡W). This kind of menu item acts like a switch, turning something on and off. In the computer jargon this is sometimes referred to as 'toggling' between two different states ie wrap on and wrap off. Your Psion Series 3 starts life with wrap off. I personally prefer wrap on because I find it easier to take in information by scrolling down the screen rather than across on the one line. As usual your Psion Series 3 offers the choice.

> ▶Mr P Siena
> 01987 654321
> 456789
> london, new york, paris, munich
> top of the palmtops

When you are in Find mode and don't intend to add data for a while, it may be worth turning the labels off. This provides a bit more room on screen although sometimes the labels are needed for clarity.

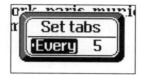

You can press the Tab key to format text within your field. Each tab press moves four character spaces by default but this can be adjusted with Display/Set tabs (∪T).

Make sure you have enough fields from the beginning. If you have to add fields later then you can only add at the end of the record without causing existing fields and their respective information to become mismatched.

Identifier

At the design stage you may wish to consider using one label (field) as a means of identifying the record in a particular category. For instance, you may wish to devise a set of codes which represent the status of the record. These could be 'keywords' of your own devising or they may be keywords which mean something in your specialism or industry.

I've been using my Psion Series 3 for recording stock levels in a warehouse so I've chosen to use the stock codes for the items I'm counting. Perhaps you are collecting information which needs to have a time attached to it. You could use a standard time/day/month format in a field so that you could search for information by days of the week, or months of the year or time of day.

It is possible to use the Find mode described above on a single field so, even in a large collection of records, looking up an entry in this way can be pretty quick. Press Menu and choose Search/Find by label (⌵S). A little dialogue pops up.

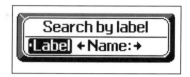

You don't want to search by all labels so press the arrow keys to step through each label in turn. When you get to the label whose information you wish to search then press Enter and the name of the label appears down in the bottom left-hand corner in place of the usual Find: prompt. Type some text and Enter to search in the normal fashion described above.

Getting it Down

As discussed elsewhere, it's difficult to type quickly on the Psion keyboard, especially if you have a telephone in one hand! Keep your colleague talking and get the information down. If you have a Series 3c or Siena then use Jotter to type in the information and then copy and insert it into the relevant fields inside Data.

If you jot notes on paper, you'll inevitably forget to transfer it to your Psion and this defeats the point. Once it's on your Psion, it's also only one step from your desktop PC via PsiWin (see the PsiWin chapter later). If you do have problems getting info down quickly then the voice memo may be an answer for temporarily storing, say, name and address information. Check out the chapter on recording, replaying and using messages.

Exporting

Information is valuable so you may wish to use it in places other than in Data itself. If you wish to use an item of a Data record in another Psion Series 3 application then you can copy it (⌵C) and then go to the 'target' application and choose Edit/Bring text to insert the text at the cursor.

You'll see in the chapter on PsiWin that Data files can be transferred to an equivalent application running under Windows. This holds the Data information in the same format and does pretty much the same job, acting as a sort of 'QuickDEX' – the card-based office record keeping system.

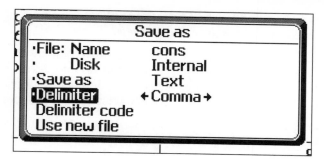

Exporting large amounts of information to other applications, both in and out of the Psion Series 3, is done via the Save as (⌴A) dialogue. Type in a name for your export file. This should be different from the filename of the any other database. You may wish to use some reminder in the name that this is an export file. Our 'Contacts' file might become 'ConsEx' or something similar.

Choose the Disk to which you wish to save and in Save as, change Data to Text. Data is the 'native' format of Psion Data, which won't be recognised by the target application. Text is standard ASCII characters which all applications can recognise and load, although not necessarily make sense of.

The Limit

Under Delimiter you have a choice of Newline, Tab, Comma, Semicolon, Other. If you choose Other then the Delimiter code field below becomes active and you can choose the code you are going to use to separate your field data. The most common delimiter is certainly a comma, which is usually placed between fields. A Newline character is commonly used to represent the end of a record and the format of the file produced is a common one known as Comma Separated Value (CSV). You can import such files into many applications, including Access and Excel on a desktop PC.

We'll view the resultant file in the next chapter. In the meantime you'll have to take my word for it that the file contains each field which contains information plus a comma.Each record begins on a new line. This format can be imported into any database in the world without difficulty.

Database Design

All applications handle data of some sort or another but databases have the job of organising it for a useful life in your computer. Useful is the operative word here. However much data you can collect, it's not much use if you can't access it in the way you wish. And so the first piece of advice when considering data handling on the Psion Series 3 is to think through how you will want to access any information you gather.

The sort of questions that are relevant are: how quickly do I want the information? In what form do I want it, chopped up into fields, in chunks of text, ready for export to another application? How much data can I store on my system? Do I want to protect my data from inspection by others?

Your main design tool in Data is the Edit labels option with which you can order the fields of information. In PsiWin there's an identical Data program so you can use the same record cards on your desktop PC. Data has many limitations when it comes to serious database work so you may wish to consider other commercial databases which are available for the Psion Series 3. Make a checklist of what you require and then check it against the available commercial software.

Summary

Data can be used to enter items of information in a record format which can have as many different labels of your choice as there are lines. Over 4,000 characters (approximately 800 words) can be entered in one record although only a fraction can be viewed on screen at one time. Strings of characters can be searched for in the database in order to pick up particular records. Ideal for collecting data, Data has very restricted facilities for manipulating the information in the form of grouping records into subsets, producing reports or sorting. However you can record information in the Psion Series 3 and can export it to a more powerful database on a desktop computer if that's what you need.

Chapter 14

....

Filing System

 In Chapters Four and Five you learned how to rename, delete and copy files which appear on the System screen. You also learned about how applications save files and how they can be reopened from within the application or from the System screen. Underlying the actions you carried out is the Psion Series 3's *filing system*.

Below you'll learn to use further aspects of the filing system, both in and out of the System screen. It's therefore a good moment for me to describe a filing system and its uses so that the following explanations of individual functions make a bit more sense.

Filing System

The Psion Series 3 filing system is based on that of MSDOS, the disk operating system which is available on desktop PCs. If you have used this system then you will recognise some of the following explanations. If not, the next few paragraphs will provide background to the actions you are going to carry out on your files.

Hierarchical

You Psion Series 3 supports what is called a hierarchical filing system which means that it can have several levels. At this point it's probably worth drawing an analogy.

Picture your desk at home, in the office or at school and imagine that you have no access to filing cabinets, drawers or cupboards. You would have to keep every single book and sheet of paper on top of your desk. This would produce a cluttered area which would be difficult to work in and would raise your blood pressure whenever you tried to locate a particular item. In an organised

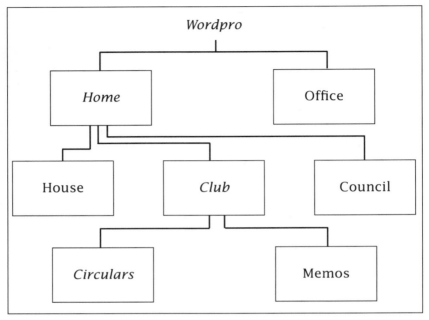

Figure 14.1. Hierarchical filing system.

working environment you would arrange your books and papers into folders or drawers which themselves would be held in a desk or filing cabinet.

Your Psion Series 3 is your filing cabinet and its directories are the equivalent of the folders/drawers. Directories can be used as a means of organising your files. You can create a directory, give it a name and then place the relevant files inside it. For instance, you may wish to use your Psion Series 3 as a wordprocessor and as a means to write letters for both home and work. You could create two directories and label them Home and Work. You could then save each file you create in the relevant directory.

You can also go a step further. Directories may themselves contain other directories. Let's take the Home directory a step further. You might find that you are producing several types of documents. For example, House, Club, Council. You could create these named directories inside the Home directory and then place the relevant files in the appropriate directories. And we could take it a step further again. You might create two types of wordprocessor files for your Club – namely Circulars and Memos. Once again these directories could be created and used in similar fashion. In fact there is no limit to the number of directories that can be placed or nested inside other directories, subject to there being enough space on your disk to do so.

It is quite common to refer to directories stored inside other directories as sub-directories. Figure 14.1 opposite illustrates the scenario outlined above. Examine this carefully to see just how this hierarchy works.

The thing that should become immediately apparent from arranging your files in this way is that it makes it very easy to locate files when you next want them. If you want a Club memo file you'll know exactly where to look!

The Tree Structure

Because of the Figure's arrangement, it is sometimes called a tree directory. You can imagine the various sub-directories being the roots of a tree, or if you turn the lot upside down, the branches of a tree. The very top of the tree structure, ie the top directory (this is the one that is displayed when you open a disk icon) is normally referred to as the root directory for this reason. The root directory of your disk is the one that you see when you first double-click on its icon.

If you look down the structure of the Home directory you will notice that several directories are on the same level but they are not connected directly. For instance, the directories House, Club and Council are all sub-directories of Home but there is no direct connection between them other than via the Home directory. This is a very important concept and one that you should fully understand.

Imagine you are working on a file stored in the Club directory. This is called the current directory. To go to the Council directory you must first go to Home (ie up the directory tree) before moving to Council. There are absolutely no shortcuts!

Parent and Child

A sub-directory can also be referred to as the child of the parent directory in which it is located. Thus in the Figure, Home is both the child of the Wordprocessing Drawer and the parent of House directory.

Directory Paths

When you need to reference a particular file you can do so by giving what is called its path name. The path name consists of the file name preceded by any directories and sub-directories which must be accessed to reach it. Each directory name is separated by a slash character. So to write the path name of a file called August in the Circulars directory in the Figure we would use:

RAMDRIVE:\Wordprocessing\Home\Club\Circulars\August

The last name is generally a file and not a directory. Also it isn't always required that you give the disk name in the root if the disk to be used is implied, in which case the path name would become:

\Wordprocessing\Home\Club\Circulars\August

This terminology can be applied to any disk you use on your Psion Series 3. Note that a colon : has been used here to separate the disk name from the directories. This is how the Psion Series 3 recognises that you are referring to a disk and not a directory or directory.

Creating a directory structure is an exercise worth taking some time over. Think about where programs should belong. Do you create a wordprocessing directory or simply use the default WRD directory, which is where Word saves its files automatically. Do you like to group programs under their function, perhaps together with the data files with which they work, or by category, so that you put all the programs into one directory and all the data files into another.

Data Files

We mentioned earlier that when you do a Save As (∪A) and give a name, an application, such as Data, saves the file in a place of its own choosing on the Internal drive. In the normal course of things you view this file through the Data program and can operate on the file from the System screen. We'll now go and have a look DAT which is where Data saves its database files and you can now see the Contacts file which you saved earlier.

PsiGuide begins... Moving around directories

Make sure you are in the System screen.

Use the arrow keys to highlight Data. Press Tab to reveal a listing of the files in the DAT directory.

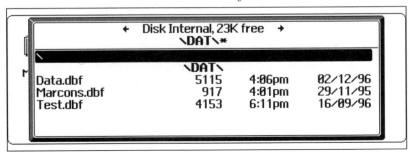

You are now in the file selector which has taken its cue from your highlighting Data in the System screen. You can use the file selector to move around directories.

You can get to the file selector by pressing Tab from the System screen or by pressing Tab when you are in a Save as dialogue inside an application.

The file selector will start you off in a position appropriate to the application from which you came.

Press the up arrow key twice to highlight the \ character. Press Enter to see a new list with DAT highlighted.

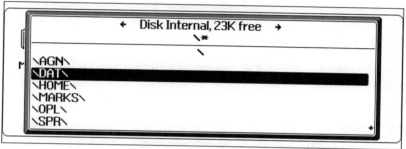

You have moved 'up' the directory tree from DAT to \. The root directory, the 'top' directory is represented by the \ character.

Try moving up to the centred \ character above and pressing Enter. You get the message 'Choose a filename.' You can go no further 'up' the tree. You can go 'down' however.

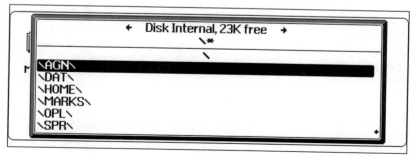

Use the down arrow key to highlight \AGN\ and press Enter to move down into AGN and to see the files which reside there.

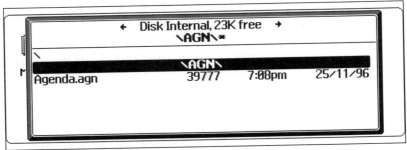

PsiGuide ends

Note the difference between this \ character and the more common / character. Make sure you use \ in your file names.

You can also operate on files from within the file selector. Press Menu to see a File menu and a Directory menu.

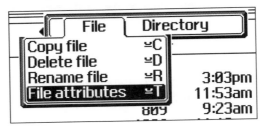

File/File attributes (∪T) is where you can resurrect hidden files to the System screen. If you have set a file attribute to Hidden Yes then the file name will not appear below its application in the System screen. You'll need to visit the file's directory, highlight it and change its attribute back to Hidden No.

PsiGuide begins... Reviving a hidden file

It's often useful to hide a file from the System screen, either to tidy up or to keep it private. If you haven't already done this then choose File/File attributes (⊔T) from the System screen and change the attributes of one of your files.

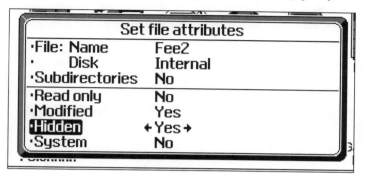

From the System screen, highlight another file from the appropriate application and press Tab. In this example, the file is from Sheet so we are working within the SPR directory and the files within.

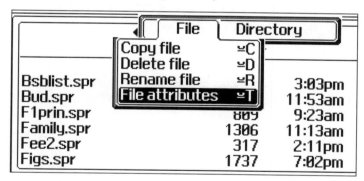

Choose File/File attributes (⊔T) and choose Hidden No. You are returned to the system screen and, hey presto, the file is back on screen in the list beneath the Word application.

If you are creating a lot of files for one application then making them hidden when they are not in use can speed up using the System screen to select active files.

PsiGuide ends

Directory Details

Let's take a closer look at the information contained in the AGN directory we ended up inside in our first PsiGuide. The top line contains a description of the disk on which the 'agenda.agn' file is stored. You can see it on the System screen but it is actually stored on the internal disk of the Psion Series 3. This disk, also referred to as RAMDRIVE, is an area of computer memory set aside for storing files and the file management software of the Psion Series 3 lets you perform tasks with and on these files.

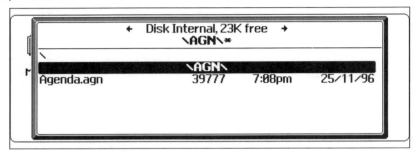

The default files which are listed beneath the Psion Series 3 applications are all stored on the internal disk of course and any new files you create will also find a home here. It has a limited capacity, like all computer memory.

If you intend to store large amounts of information on your Psion Series 3 then its memory can be expanded to cope. Details on expansion options appear in the appropriate appendix at the end of this book.

For now the top line of the display shows that there are 20K of free space on the internal disk. Computer memory is measured in K and you need to know approximately what the figures your Psion Series 3 displays mean.

One K is made up of 1,024 bytes and it's a reasonable approximation to say that one byte is the equivalent of one character in a document. 2K then is about enough for a 2,000 character document, say 400 words or so. These are very rough approximations but may help in your judgement of how much memory your Psion Series 3 tasks will require.

The second line of the screen shows the directory path on display. It's the AGN directory, shown after one \ character and before another \. The first \ signifies that AGN is one level down from the top level of the filing system. The second \ is followed by an asterisk (*) which signifies that 'all' the files in AGN are displayed below.

AGN is a 'directory', a named area where files can be stored. The file display window above is 'live' and you can use the arrow keys to highlight the entries in turn. the one file 'Agenda.agn' should be highlighted. The three bits of information to the right are called 'fields' and contain:

> **the file size in bytes (32389)**
>
> **the time the file was created**
>
> **the date the file was created**

Press the up arrow key to highlight \AGN\ and press Enter. A help message in the bottom right-hand corner asks you to choose a filename. that's because you are already in the AGN directory and hence selecting it achieves nothing.

File Menu

That's the background to how files are organised. Now it's time to complete your knowledge of the various functions you can carry out on and with files. Press the Esc key to return to the System screen and then use the Menu key to follow this tour of menu options.

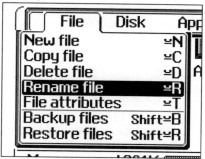

Copy, Delete, Rename

We looked at these functions in an earlier chapter. However we didn't use them in tandem with the directory structure, which is my cue for a PsiGuide to show you how.

PsiGuide begins... Copying a file

Move to Word on the System screen and press Tab. Press Menu and choose Directory/Make directory (^ +) and type in HOME.

On returning to System, press Tab again to see the \WRD\HOME\ directory in position. Use the arrow keys to highlight a file you wish to copy and press Menu.

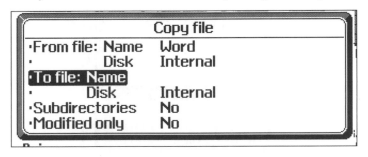

Choose Copy file (∪C). In the resulting dialogue you'll see the filename on the top line. Arrow key down twice so that the cursor is flashing in the To file: Name field.

```
                      Copy file
·From file: Name    Word
·          Disk     Internal
·To file: Name
·          Disk     Internal
·Subdirectories     No
·Modified only      No
```

Press the Tab key. In the file selector which pops up, use the arrow keys to highlight the \WRD\HOME\ directory and press Enter.

You have 'navigated' into the HOME directory. Press Enter again. You'll see the pathname displayed briefly in the bottom right-hand corner.

Now type the name of the file into the To file: Name field. Just copy the name in the From file: Name field above. The two names won't clash because the copy is going to be in the HOME directory.

PsiGuide ends

File Selector

You've now encountered the file selector in a number of different guises: whether it's used in the System screen, in the filing system menus or in an application Save as dialogue box, it acts as a 'window' on the directory structure. It's the main way that you can look around the directories and specify a 'destination' directory for a file.

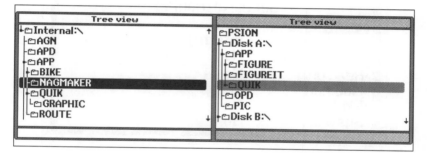

Series 3c owners have a file manager which provides the features we've been working on but with the advantage of an easy to use 'tree' display. The twin window display may be familiar to you from your desktop PC.

The Series 3c file manager provides the File and Disk functions which are also available on the System screen but you can use the arrow keys to move around the tree structure to operate directly on files.

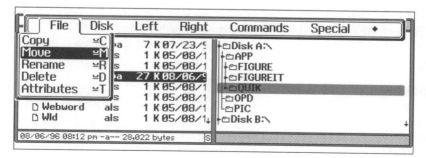

In the next chapter we'll take a look at the drag and drop features of PsiWin on a desktop PC. If you are a PsiWin user then it can make sense to keep any complex filing operations until you are in Psion File Manager when you can do them all in a batch, using the drag and drop features of that software.

Attributes

File attributes is the next option in the File menu. It brings up a dialogue which gives some control over the way a file can be treated by the filing system. We've already seen how the Hidden field can be used. The Read only Yes/No setting is important if you are concerned about protecting a particular file from change or deletion.

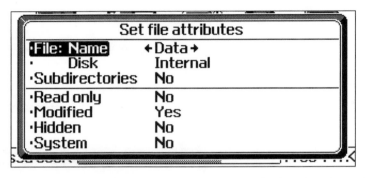

For instance, if you've finished your biology project in Word and you have to give your Psion Series 3 to someone else before you have a chance to print out your work. You might feel happier selecting your file and setting the Read only attribute to Yes, which means someone can look at your work but they can't modify the file containing it.

The Modified attribute is used by the backing-up software so that you can restrict your back-ups to files which have actually changed since the last time. If a file's System attribute is set to Yes then you know that the file is something to do with an application and this should not be changed. There is also no point in setting non System files to System unless you have embarked on some programming to create your own applications.

Backing Up and Restoring

Losing data is possible so taking a copy of your files (backing-up) is a good thing. It can't be stated too often or too strongly: back up your data regularly and thoroughly. Because your Psion Series 3 memory will begin to contain important system files and your resources will be ordered as you want them, it is important to backup.

As well as regular complete backups, it's not a bad idea to backup specific work in progress. If you have just completed a day's work, say a spreadsheet or a small program, then a few minutes backing up the file or the relevant directory is excellent value in terms of insurance.

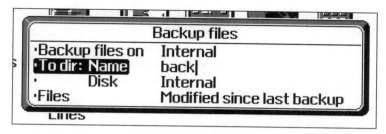

Backup and Restore files are the Psion Series 3's insurance policy in case something zaps the memory and you're left to not have a nice day. However you can only make use of these utilities if you have a second disk. An alternative to using a second Psion disk is to use PsiWin to backup to a desktop PC (see the chapter on PsiWin). You can back-up All or files Modified since last backup.

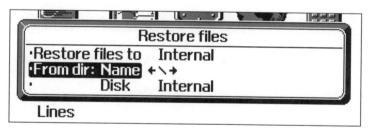

Restore is then used to bring back the last backup you made. Be careful not to restore an old version of your files by mistake. You should normally only use Restore if you have had a major loss of data.

Using the Copy command to copy files to another disk is an alternative way of 'backing up' your work. By having it on a separate disk, it provides peace of mind in case the internal disk should lose data. A quick way to backup a number of files is to use copy on a whole directory and its subdirectories.

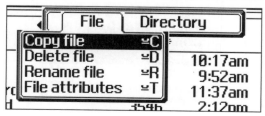

To do this you need to drop down into the filing system by pressing Tab, move to the level above the directory you wish to copy and highlight it with the arrow keys before choosing Copy from the cut-down filing menu which is offered here.

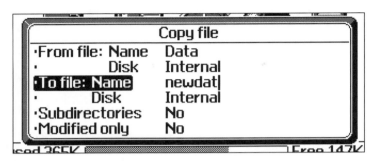

In the dialogue box choose Subdirectories Yes to force Copy to take all the material inside the highlighted directory to the destination disk.

File Menu Dialogues

In any of these commands, if the disk chosen is absent then the From: Name will contain (No disk) so that you can't select a filename from the System screen.

It's not possible to type in a file pathname in either from: or to: lines. This is when you use the Tab key to move to the destination directory. Although the dialogue only displays the filename, it uses the directory to which you've 'navigated' with the file selector.

If you choose to use the name of a disk which doesn't physically exist in the Psion Series 3 then the Absent message will appear in the bottom right-hand corner of your screen. Choose another disk and try again.

Disk

We continue our look at the filing system with the Disk menu.

Directory (↻*)

This command (↻*) or (Tab) shows you the files in the directory you have highlighted. If you've highlighted a Word file then the WRD directory is shown. Once in the filing system you can move around and look at files and carry out operations on them. See the explanation of the filing system above.

Make directory (↻+)

This offers a dialogue which prompts for a directory name. It doesn't tell you this on screen, not until it's too late anyway, but the directory is created inside the current directory on the internal disk. So, if you are already in WRD then the new directory will appear inside the WRD directory. It won't appear on the System screen.

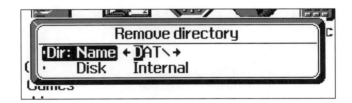

Remove directory (↻-)

Be careful with this one because it lists the major directories on your Psion Series 3 and you don't really want to lose any of them. Think hard before using this option!

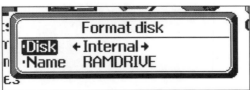

Format disk (↻F)

Watch out here too! This command will wipe everything on your disk. If you get to the dialogue by mistake, press the Esc key.

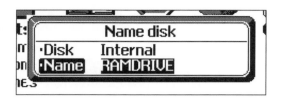

Name disk (◡H)

If you strongly dislike your internal disk being called RAMDRIVE then change it. Otherwise, leave it alone.

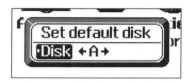

Default disk (Shift ◡H)

If you have a SSD disk then you can make it the default (usual) disk for your filing activities.

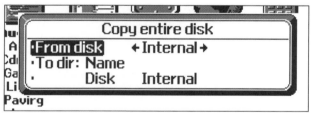

Copy disk (Shift ◡C)

This copies an entire disk – all files and directories and subdirectories – to a destination which will, common sense tells us, be another disk. The dialogue allows you to copy a whole disk into a directory on another disk. You need to judge for yourself if enough space is available in the destination.

Naming Conventions

I mentioned briefly in an earlier chapter that choosing filenames for your files is worth spending a few moments on. It's not especially easy to use the directory structure of the Psion Series 3 to organise large numbers of files so using consistent naming conventions is a possible alternative means of organisation and recognition.

There are a number of approaches. The filename can contain an abbreviation indicating who to or what for. Letters and memos can have the first three letters of the surname of the person to whom the document is to be sent. For reports or forms, use the first three letters of a significant word in the title.

The date a file is created is clearly displayed by the Psion Series 3 in its directory and file display so this can be left to the system. If you are making the document available (posting) to colleagues then you may wish to add a three character signature as the originator. A spreadsheet from Mark Owen Webb would be called spredMOW. Note that I've chosen to misspell the spread to squeeze the filename into the available eight characters, but I've retained the sound of the word. This is a way of remembering what it represents.

The file extension is used by the system to specify the type of the file and this should be left to the Psion Series 3 to decide upon so that translations to other formats can be successfully carried out.

Recognising files for what they are can be very handy when tidying up the memory of your Psion Series 3. You can be selective in archiving files to SSD or, via PsiWin, to PC disk. These files can be retained just in case, but you don't want them cluttering up your precious memory. You can use the files' dates to decide whether to archive or you can keep your templates and standard documents while archiving all general correspondence and old reports etc. A sensible and consistent naming system which works for you will make this level of organisation possible.

Chapter 15

....

Organising Numbers

 The third program in the holy trinity of computing is the spreadsheet. A spreadsheet is a program designed to manipulate numbers. Because we've all got a small screen area in which to view information, it is difficult to describe the scope of a spreadsheet. If you've played a platform computer game then you'll be aware that it contains many different screens, above, below and side by side each other but only one screen is displayed at a time. In the same way, the spreadsheet is a large sheet of ruled paper containing many screen-size chunks of information, which can only be viewed one screenfull at a time.

The blank sheet can usually be as big as you'll ever need, certainly big enough for home accounts, a work schedule, even small business accounts. The sheet is ruled vertically and horizontally, usually with about 10 text characters between each vertical line and one character height between each horizontal line. The rectangles enclosed by these lines are known as *cells* and it is in each cell that you place information, either text or numbers.

Start up Sheet now by pressing its icon, and pressing Enter if there is not already a sheet open for use. Use a blank sheet to try out some of the ideas which follow in this chapter.

You can enter a number by activating a cell and typing the number into it. The cursor starts up in the cell in the top left-hand corner of the sheet. The cursor here is represented by the cell having a dark box around it. We refer to this cell as A1. The cell to its right is B1 and the cell below it is A2. You'll notice that the cell reference is displayed in the top left-hand corner of the Sheet display.

Use the arrow keys to move down a couple of rows and type in the number 500 and press Enter. The number appears in the cell and you'll see it in the 'line editor' at the top of the screen.

As well as a number, you can type in a formula. For instance, move the cursor down onto the next row and type:

4+3

and press Enter to cause the result 7 to appear in the cell. Arrow key down a row and type:

4*3

and Enter, which will appear in the cell as 12. The * (asterisk) is used to mean *multiply* in spreadsheet formulae.

Entering Formulae

Sheet distinguishes between two ways of entering formulae. The first is demonstrated above. Move up to the cell into which you typed 4+3 and you will see 7 appear in the line editor above. Now type in

=4+3

and press Enter. The number 7 appears as before but now when you move onto the cell the line editor above will still contain the formula =4+3. It makes most sense to use this second version with the equals sign preceding the formula. This is because you never know when you might wish to edit the formula at a later stage.

The value in a cell is available for use in another cell, using the grid reference method. For example:

C3-5

which means take the value in cell C3 and subtract 5. C3 means the cell which appears three in from the left - A, B, C - and three down from the top - 1, 2, 3.

This is the grid reference method which is used to refer to any cell in the sheet. When a large sheet gets to Z, it continues with AA, AB, AC etc.

Range

If the spreadsheet cell is the atom then the range is the molecule. A range is a group of cells, rectangular in shape, defined by reference to the top left-hand and bottom right-hand cells contained within it.

In Sheet you can define a range by highlighting it, which is achieved by holding down the Shift key and moving the cursor with the arrow keys. The highlighted cells constitute a range and a number of menu operations use this as an area to work on.

Relative and Absolute

The formula given above C3-5 is a relative to the cell it is in. If you copy this formula, the reference C3 will change to refer to another cell in the same relative position to the cell in which the formula resides. If you wish to make C3 refer to C3 even when it is copied, enter the formula like this:

C3-5

which makes the formula absolute. Wherever you copy this formula, the C3 reference will remain.

Text

Text entries are more important than you might think in a numbers program because they are needed to describe and document the numbers, whose meaning you would soon forget if they were left on their own, unlabelled.

You can type text into any cell you wish. If you want to set the alignment from the outset then use the following prefix characters in Table 15.1.

Character	Action
'	left align
^	centre
"	right align
\	fill cell with copies of text

Table 15.1. Text alignment prefixes

Imagine a colleague at work finding a sheet full of figures on your desk. The figures wouldn't mean much unless there were quite detailed descriptions. Text can also be used to present the numbers in the spreadsheet in the form of a report. You can do this in Sheet, or it may be that you will export (save in a standard format) the numbers for use in your wordprocessor.

While moving around Sheet, there are a number of useful hot-key shortcuts which you can use (Table 15.2).

Action	Key press
Edit cell	Enter
Delete cell contents	Delete
Highlight column	Control Tab
Highlight row	Control Space
Cancel highlight	Esc
Move to cell A1	Control ∪ left arrow key
Move one screenfull up/down	∪ up/down arrow keys
Move one screenfull left/right	∪ left/right arrow keys
Move to top/bottom edge of extent	Control up/down arrow keys
Move to left/right edge of extent	Control left/right arrow keys
Step down column, in range	Control Enter
Move left/right with wrap, in range	Tab/Shift Tab

Table 15.2. Shortcuts cut down on key presses.

Sheet Menus – Filing

Let's work our way through what Sheet has to offer, menu by menu. The first three menus are fairly straightforward and will be familiar by now.

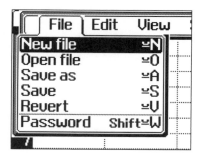

File/New file (∪N) creates a new blank sheet. A dialogue provides a field for the name of your new sheet to be typed in, together with a choice of location (Internal disk and so on). When you've completed the creation of a new file, any file already open disappears and the best way back to it is to exit the new file and enter the old by selecting it from the list under Sheet in the System screen.

Open file (∪O) offers a dialogue from which you can select an existing spreadsheet file.

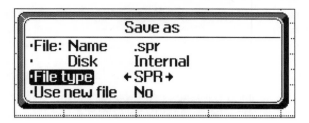

The 'Save as' (∪A) menu pops up a four line dialogue for name, location, filetype and 'Use new file'. The filetypes on offer are:

SPR – the native Sheet spreadsheet format.

WKI – Lotus compatible format.

WKS – Lotus compatible format.

DIF – general spreadsheet format for export (loses underlying formulae).

If you want to use the newly created file (because Save as creates a new file under your new name) straightaway then make sure that you select

Use new file Yes

in the dialogue. This will also have the effect of suspending the file you were working on until you select it again from the System screen.

If you want to save your file anywhere other than in the default directory of SPR then press Tab when you are in the Save as dialogue and move to the directory you wish to save into. See the chapter on Filing System for more detail on using the File selector in this way.

Save (∪S) saves any changes you've made recently to the file on disk. If no changes have occurred since the last save then a message will advise you.

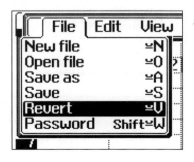

The Revert option quickly gets you out of a spot if you've made an error and the best course of action is simply to go back to the sheet you started with. This option reloads your last saved version. Bearing this in mind, it is a good policy not to save in the middle of an action which you think may go wrong, giving you an option to Revert to the position before your experiment began.

Alternatively if you're trying out new or 'en-masse' changes to your sheet then why not 'save as' under a new name before proceeding. You can then Open the old file if things really go haywire, and delete the new one later.

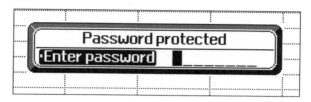

Password (Shift⌣W) brings up a dialogue into which you type a password up to eight characters long and then confirm it below. Pressing Enter and saving the file completes the password protection. You now need the password to Open the sheet or to change the password again. When you try either of these actions, you get the message 'Password protected, Enter password'. You can throw away the password protection by Exit, lose changes (Shift⌣X) before saving the file or just in case you forget your wife's mother's maiden name in the meantime!

Chopping and Changing

Edit/Copy and Paste work in tandem to copy cell entries around the sheet.

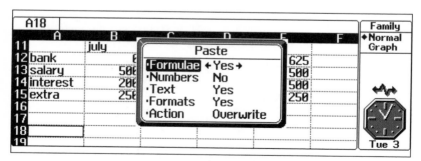

Select cells using Shift and the arrow keys and ⌣C to copy to the clipboard. Move the cursor to the cell position where you want the copy to go and ⌣I to paste the clipboard contents in. There's no delete option on this menu. If you want to delete a cell or range of cells, go to Range/Clear (∪K).

Bring is the equivalent of Paste but it only works if you've already copied something to the clipboard from another program. Unfortunately Calc has no copy to clipboard feature but, let's say you want to copy some details from a stock database. Each item can be copied to the clipboard from its card in Data (update entry) and Bring used in Sheet to paste the details into place. Just switch to and fro' the programs by pressing the respective icons on the front of your Psion Series 3.

Paste special (Shift∪I) is an important feature of the spreadsheet. It allows you to control how data is copied about. You can choose to paste the formulae you've copied or just the result. Using the Paste dialogue you can leave labels and formats behind but keep the data or, vice versa, copy a neatly created set of labels and formats to another location ready for new numbers to be entered.

PsiGuide begins… Paste special

A11						
	A	B	C	D	E	F
8	heatlit	100				
9	tax	150				
10	subtotal	1175				
11		july	aug	sep	oct	
12	bank	0	-225	1650	1625	
13	salary	500	500	400	500	
14	interest	200	2300	500	500	
15	extra	250	250	250	250	
16						

Family
◆Normal
Graph

Tue 3

Select a range and copy it to the clipboard (∪C). Then move to another part of your worksheet or create a new one. Position the cursor where you wish to paste the range and choose Paste special (S∪I).

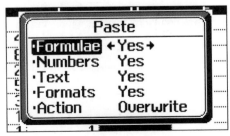

Paste

·Formulae	◄ Yes ►
·Numbers	Yes
·Text	Yes
·Formats	Yes
·Action	Overwrite

Choose the options you want from the dialogue to control what data is carried across in the paste process.

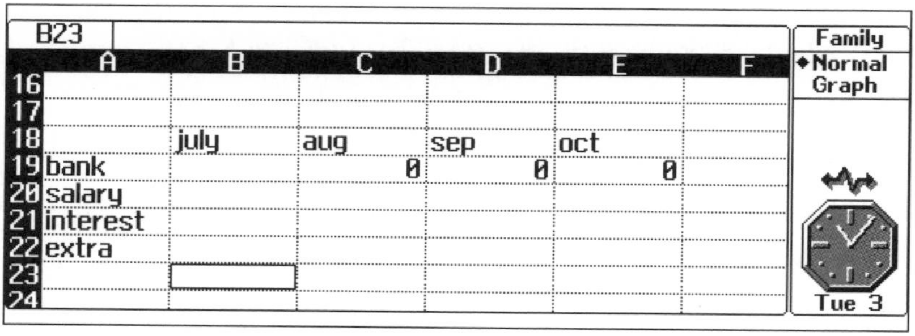

B23						Family
						◆ Normal
	A	B	C	D	E	F	Graph

Row labels and contents:
- 16
- 17
- 18 · july · aug · sep · oct
- 19 bank · · 0 · 0 · 0
- 20 salary
- 21 interest
- 22 extra
- 23
- 24

Tue 3

The result is a new range copied from the original but modified for re-use. You can copy the format without the numbers or the numbers without the format, and so on.

Opening and Closing

You'll find that new information has to be added to your sheet or a column or row needs to be removed. Open/close gap (Shift⌒O) is the means to these ends. Use the arrow keys to highlight the relevant area and then press Shift⌒O. The Open/close dialogue provides for all the combinations:

To do	Action	Move
Insert row	Open	Down
Insert column	Open	Right
Remove row	Close	Up
Remove column	Close	Left

Experiment with these before trying anything on a large spreadsheet you value. The key is to define the area carefully with the arrow keys before opening or closing a gap. If it goes wrong you can fall back on Undo (⌒U) to reopen or close up again.

Normally you won't need Recalc (⌒-) because recalculation is going on all the time. If you've turned recalculation off (which should only ever be necessary for very large sheets) then this becomes a means of updating your spreadsheet after you've changed a value or formula which effects other cells in the sheet. It just prompts Sheet to make sure all the calculations are up to date.

View Menu

Format applies one of the formats to a single cell, a range of cells or the whole sheet (default).

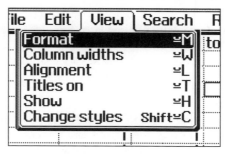

You can define a range with Shift and the arrow keys before choosing the option (⌐M). If you haven't defined a range in this way or you've changed your mind, you can type the range into the Range field in the form: top left cell reference: bottom right cell reference. These two cell references act to define the rectangle of cells which is the range. Show as offers the following choice of formats:

General	Date
Time	Hidden
Show Formulae	Bargraph
Default	Fixed
Scientific	Currency
Percent	Triad

You can specify the number of decimal places in the last five of these formats, up to 15 decimal places.

The final field is Font, which offers a choice of four styles as defined in the Change styles menu. The default styles are plain, italic, bold and bold/italic. These give you some scope for presenting your information attractively.

Let's take a further look at what you can achieve by applying the above formats.

Date

This is designed for calendar dates and it derives its format form the Time/Settings/Formats dialogue where the order of day, month and year can be set and the separator defined. The Time format comes from here too. Date can give some interesting results when applied to single numbers.

Hidden

This removes the information in a cell from the display. Moving the cursor over the cell reveals that the information is still there. Use this to tidy away 'workings' which you don't wish to show or to simplify the layout on display to clarify the meaning of what you have in front of you.

Show Formulae

This exposes the workings behind the values, which is useful when developing your spreadsheet. You can also print out the whole sheet with formulae instead of values, if you need an overview of the spreadsheet's structure (Special/Print).

	A	B	C	D	E	F
6						
7	beer consumption					
8	XXX	▨	stout lad	▨	mild	▨
9	old cloudy	▨	smoothy	▨	gelbpils	▨
10						
11	*******	*******	*******	*******	*******	******
12						

Bargraph

This isn't the same as Graph but generates a mini graph within each cell it's applied to. If dry numbers aren't appropriate then a shaded bar can do the trick. For instance to show the number of pints of different beers drunk at a real ale festival.

Default

Any format can be set as default in the Format dialogue and it is then applied through this setting.

Fixed

This offers the chance to have some decimal places. Scientific format is a way of expressing very large or very small numbers. There's a discussion on this in the chapter on Calc.

Currency

This is very useful because spreadsheets often have something to do with money. The currency format takes its definition from the System/Control/Number formats dialogue so you only work in one currency at a time, using the format. There's no problem in defining your own label together with a value for more than one national currency. You can then reference the relevant cell to make a conversion.

Percent

This takes .01 and turns it into 1%, .1 into 10% and so on.

Triad

This is the same as fixed but with a comma separator between every three digits.

On Display

You don't normally need to adjust column widths (∪W) but some text and perhaps formulae will inevitably be too wide for the default 8 character cell width. In the case of a title this needn't matter because the text will simply flow into and over other empty cells.

When you have adjoining cells containing data which overlap then some adjustment may be required. You can change the cells in the column in which you are working or you can define a range through Shift and arrow keys or by typing into the Columns field in the form start column:end column. You can also use the Set column width dialogue to Action Restore to put the widths back to 8 characters across. If you wish to effect the whole sheet then use Alter Default.

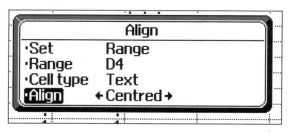

Alignment similarly works on a range (Set Range) or the whole sheet Set Default). The range is defined with Shift and arrow keys or by typing in the cell references (see above). Cell type can be Text or Numeric. Under Numeric the cell contents can be aligned left or right in the cell. Under Text, the choice is from left, right, centred or repeated.

The first three options can be used to neaten up the look of a sheet but should be used sparingly and with consideration. Centring may be appropriate for a title but it can look silly above a column of right-aligned numbers. Repeat repeats the text in a cell, to fill the cell width. For instance, type in a single * (asterisk) and seven asterisks will appear automatically Use this technique to 'cordon off' parts of your sheet.

Now You See It

Show (◡H) controls the display of Grid labels, lines and zero values in a Yes or No dialogue. The labels are the A, B, C and 1, 2, 3 across and down and they can be dispensed with for printing.

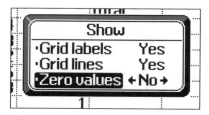

The grid lines help the eye match up columns correctly so are arguably more useful. They too can go if you've introduced other visual guides such as bar graphs and repeating characters. Zero values in cells can occur and this decides on displaying or not.

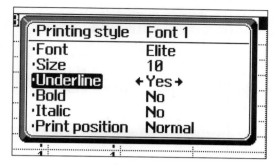

Change styles (Shift∪C) offers you the opportunity to edit the four standard styles available in Sheet – see Format above. You can choose outrageous definitions – Arial 50 point underlined – but they won't display on scree, but they will print out so watch out and use Print preview just in case!

Search Menu

Find is useful because it's easy to lose track of where you've put things in a growing spreadsheet.

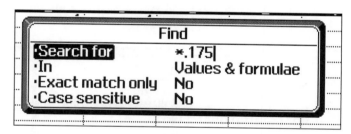

You can search in Values only, Formulae only or in both, and restrict yourself to exact matching and to case sensitivity if you wish. The cursor highlights the cell which contains the first match and pressing ∪G (Find again) moves to the next match, if there is one.

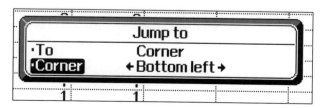

Jump to (∪J) is a sort of transporter to any cell position, using To Range/Cell, or a quick jump to one of the four corners of your sheet. The former is more useful. Once you've named a range of cells (see Range/Add name below), you are offered the option to jump to a named range.

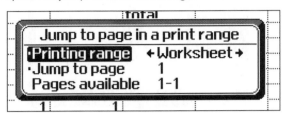

Jump to page (Shift⌣J) is useful when your sheet has grown beyond a single page, as defined by the print range (see Set print range below). When you are building a large sheet, especially one which is going to be printed in the form of a report, it is important to preplan on which page certain information is to appear. You can have a page for setting up values, another for formulae and a third for results summaries. Jumping to the appropriate page then becomes useful.

Ranges

We've already encountered the 'range' of cells and seen that, once defined, it can be acted upon as a separate entity.

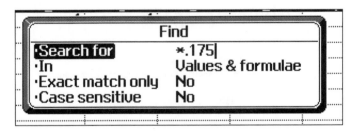

The Range menu is concerned with setting the characteristics of a range and defining print ranges.

Sort (Shift⌣S) operates on a range to bring the entries in the cells in the range into ASCII-sorted order. ASCII is alphabetic but also contains numbers and other keyboard characters which will also be sorted in any list created by this function.

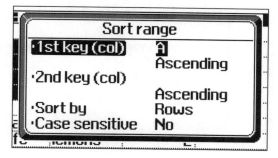

A19	'lemons	
	A	**B**
13	pears	1
14	lemons	3
15	apples	6
16	oranges	2

Typically the range will consist of a column containing text labels and columns containing numbers attached to these labels. Sort lists the labels in ASCII order, retaining the labels' links with their numbers.

Sort range	
·1st key (col)	A
	Ascending
·2nd key (col)	
	Ascending
·Sort by	Rows
·Case sensitive	No

If you wish to sort the second column of numbers, you will have to do it separately by making it the range to sort.

C	**D**
apples	1
lemons	3
oranges	6
pears	2

Use Sheet to compile text and number combinations (a book index for instance) so that you can sort them alphabetically before exporting to Word.

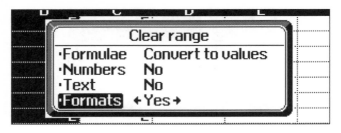

Clearing a range (∪K) provides control over Formulae, Numbers, Text and Formats so it's useful for editing a range for other purposes. Use this in conjunction with Copy and Paste to quickly construct new spreadsheets from the structures or figures contained in an existing sheet.

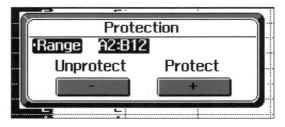

If you share your Psion Series 3 with a colleague, or you don't trust yourself, then protecting a part of your spreadsheet can ensure against accidental erasure by overtyping.

Naming a range may seem unnecessary at first but you'll appreciate any labels you can get hold of when you return to your spreadsheet and find you've forgotten quite how the numbers fit together.

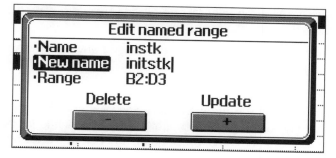

You can edit the name at any time to clarify matters in the 15 characters available and adjust the range which carries the name.

The bottom section of the Range menu is concerned with managing the print area. The sheet as designed may not fit precisely into the proportions of a piece of paper running through a printer and this is where you fit parts of the sheet to the paper format. Once print ranges have been set, you can quickly select one in the Print (∪P) dialogue.

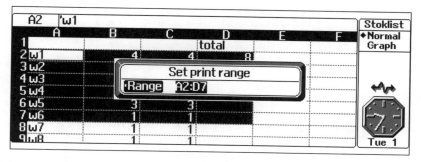

Setting a print range (Shift∪R) can be done in the same way as setting a normal range, by using Shift and the arrow keys or by typing the corner to corner definition into the dialogue.

You can set more than one print range and Sheet will take these and do its best to get them neatly printed out.

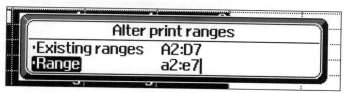

When you wish to Alter the print ranges (Shift◡E) you are offered the chance to work on more than one range at a time.

Deleting a print range (◡D) doesn't mean deleting any data in the range but simply removing the range definition.

Special

The Special menu contains the standard items plus spreadsheet's very own Set preferences and printing specifics. Let's stay with printing for the moment and then look at the other items, before jumping back to the Database menu, which we've skipped for the moment.

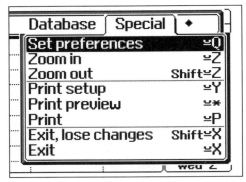

Printing from the Special menu operates on the whole worksheet or on a print range you have set.

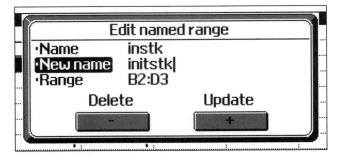

You can only print one range at a time so you can't mix a number of ranges onto one page. Plan ahead and group the data you will need to print together.

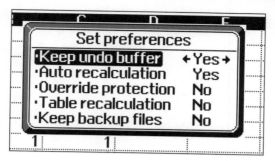

The Set preferences (∪Q) option provides control over some global priorities for the sheet. Auto recalculation can be turned off if a large sheet is recalculating slowly and holding you up. If you do turn it off and recalculation is then required, a +/- sign appears in the input line editor, at which point you can use Edit/Recalc (∪-).

We've made our way through the basic features of Sheet. Try entering some text labels and some numbers for yourself. Highlight cells and define ranges. Do a bit of copy and paste. This new familiarity with getting about Sheet and constructing spreadsheets will allow you to try out your ideas. Perhaps you want to do a family budget or keep some stock figures updated. Give it a try and then proceed to the next chapter where we'll look at some of the more advanced features which Sheet has to offer: graphs, database, tables and functions.

Chapter 16

PsiWin Your PC Connection

Perhaps the ultimate peripheral you can get for your Psion Series 3 is a PC! It's ideal for backup storage, printing and reworking your Psion Series 3 documents. If you use a PC then put it to work with PsiWin. PsiWin is a snazzy cable, called the 3Link, which connects your Psion Series 3 to the serial port of the PC plus Psion Series 3 and Windows software which.comes on three PC format floppy disks.

PsiWin is an advanced set of Windows applications which work together with a serial interface and cable. Transferring files can be a bit slower than just relying on the serial link under DOS but PsiWin's many extra features outweigh this consideration.

The idea is to integrate your Psion Series 3 fully with desktop PCs running the Windows operating system. PsiWin works with both Windows 3.1 and Windows 95 and with all Series 3 and 3a models, although Agenda conversions to PC equivalents are only valid for the Series 3a. PsiWin's advanced File Manager allows 'drag-and-drop' moving of files between your Psion and a PC.

The main things you can do with PsiWin are to move files between your Psion and your PC and to access files on the PC by the applications in the Psion. PsiWin provides a File Manager which is very similar to the Windows 3.11 File Manager, which offers comprehensive automatic back-up and flash compression facilities. It also provides a Windows database which is identical to that running on the Series 3a, allowing you to make full use of the PC's large screen and keyboard to input and maintain contacts databases. A TrueType printing utility is included to let the Psion Series 3 print to any printer connected to the PC using the full range of Windows TrueType fonts.

Connections

There's only one potential complication with connecting up your Psion Series 3 with the PsiWin cable: you've already got equipment plugged into the serial port. The standard PsiWin cable has nine pins (connections) and so the nine pin serial port on your PC needs to be free. It's unusual for a modem – the most common peripheral to use a serial connection – to use the nine pin port. However, if your PC has a mouse, it may be a serial mouse which plugs into the nine pin port, which means there's nowhere for your PsiWin connection to go. Problem!

The solution is to purchase a separate converter, into which you plug the 3Link, and which in turn you plug into the 15 pin serial port. If you have a modem connected then you'll have to swap cables between using the modem and 3Link. You can buy connecters which take two serial cables and plug them into one port, which can be more convenient and less wearing on the PC, and your back as you strain to get behind the case! You could try to run Windows without a mouse. In theory it's possible but in practice it's very difficult. All the drag and drop features are just a drag.

Most of you will not have the worry of the above but will blithely plug the 3Link cable into the nine pin port. The other end goes into the Psion Series 3 port on the left-hand side. Turn the connecter so the metal clip is facing down and in it goes.

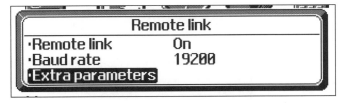

Press the System icon and choose Special/Remote link (∪L). In the dialogue use the arrow keys to choose

Remote link On

and

Baud rate 19200

Ignore Extra parameters and confirm by pressing Enter. Look at the screen just above the clock and you'll now see jagged line with arrows at either end. This shows you that Remote link is on and this graphic animates when a connection is made with another device e.g. your PC.

That's all it takes at the Psion Series 3 end so now we move over to the PC and all the screen illustrations which follow are from a PC running Windows 95. PsiWin operates equally well under Windows 3.1, Windows 3.11 for Workgroups, Windows NT and OS/2. The manual I've got states that PsiWin is for Windows 3.1 but you needn't be put off by this.

The installation procedure is typical of PC software. Insert PsiWin floppy disk one and click on Start and then Run. Type

> A:/Setup

into the space and press Enter. PsiWin takes you through the installation.

PsiGuide begins… Installing PsiWin on PC

Type A:/Setup and follow the prompts.

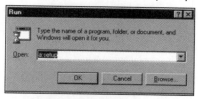

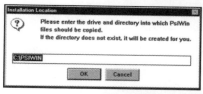 

Three disks later and you are ready to roll. Unless you've got a pressing appointment, choose to get going immediately.

PsiGuide ends

It's time for your Psion Series 3 and PC to talk to one another but first just a bit of setting up in the Communications Settings.

PsiGuide begins... Establishing communication

You should have the Communications Setting dialogue on screen. If for some reason you've dropped into the Psion Manager program then choose Settings/Communications.

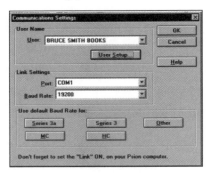

Click on the model of Psion you own e.g. Series 3a and press Enter to try to communicate with your Psion Series 3. You'll get confirmation of what's happening on your PC's screen whether it's good or bad news.

Make sure the Psion Series 3 is turned on and you should see an Updating lists and Downloading messages on the System screen. This is as it should be since the PC software is uploading some extra software to the Psion Series 3 to manage the various functions of which PsiWin is capable. When this stage is complete, PsiWin's installation procedure is over and an open window is left on screen displaying some of the PsiWin files.

PsiGuide ends

If communication is not established you'll see this message:

Don't forget the fact that the PsiWin programs are Windows programs and, as such, there's the usual Help file which you can call up from the menu bar.

What You've Got

When the installation of PsiWin is complete you'll find you've got some new folders on your PC hard drive. Installation sets up two program groups for the Psion applications. The files are held on your hard drive and a special folder @Psion is created to hold temporary and system data.

Figure 16.1. Folders, two program groups and the @Psion system folder are all created on installation.

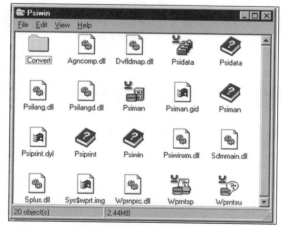

Figure 16.2. PsiWin is not one application, but many.

What you've got now is a PC and a Psion Series 3 linked together. You can't damage either by turning off either. If you do turn off the Psion Series 3 by mistake then you may lose the link temporarily. All you need to do is turn back on and double-click on PsiWin again or choose Link from the Psion menu in the Psion File Manager if it's up and running. If you've got Auto switch off On on your Psion Series 3, you might wish to change this to Off while you are using PsiWin.

File Manager

The key component in PsiWin is the File Manager, in which you gain access to the files on the PC and on the Psion. It's the equivalent utility to Microsoft's Windows 3.1 File Manager. Windows 95 users may find it a bit strange but read on and you'll get the idea.

Once the Series 3a is connected using the serial link, the File Manager provides access to all the available disk drives – the internal RAMDRIVE and, optionally, two SSD drives on the Series 3a – which are treated exactly as if they were disk drives on the PC.

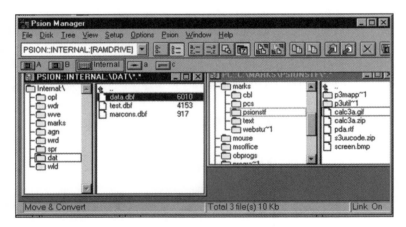

Use the Windows menu to arrange your windows so that the PC's hard disk drive (C: by default) and the Psion Series 3's disk contents are viewed side by side. Here's the key to drag and drop file copying and conversion.

All you have to do is click on the folder icons to get where you want to go in the filing system hierarchy. When you spot the file you wish to copy, drag its icon over onto the folder on the PC or Psion Series 3, depending on which direction your file is going in.

On the PC you can have folders open outside of the Psion File Manager so that you have a place to rename files and check things are going OK.

The File Manager lets you view files from different angles, by file type, size, date etc.

File Conversion

There's no point in moving files to and from your Psion and PC unless the files can be used at the other end. The way that file transfer programs achieve this is to match the files with the relevant applications and to adjust the format of the data in the file if necessary so that the application can load it. This process is called file conversion and is a vital subset of file transfer.

First things first: find the file you want to copy. Click on the appropriate Psion Series 3 disk icons and directory folders until you see the files you want, eg .wrd files in the WRD directory is where your Psion Series 3 keeps its Word wordprocessor files.

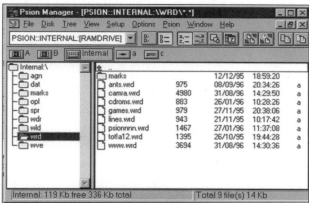

Whatever the settings in Psion File Manager, you can control what happens to a file simply by holding down a key when dragging the file to its destination.

Hold down	File action
Shift	Move a file
Ctrl	Copy a file
Alt-Shift	Move and convert a file
Alt-Ctrl	Copy and convert a file

Table 16.1. Keys which control file dragging.

When you drag a file from your Psion Series 3 RAMDRIVE to the PC's hard disk, a bar fills to indicate the copying is in progress. Psion File Manager then throws up a dialogue suggesting a file conversion.

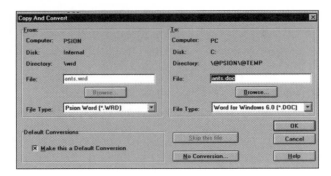

If you are copying standard files from Psion applications then you needn't study this too closely. File Manager will suggest the appropriate conversion and you need only press Enter (on the PC remember!) to agree.

A second dialogue follows, again requiring a confirming press of the Enter key. Psion File Manager settings can cut down this confirmation process.

If you are copying a file which is not 'ordinary' then you may wish to adjust the settings in the first dialogue to choose a different file conversion or none at all. You may have no choice. For instance if you drag a bitmap graphics file across to the PC you are offered a conversion to the Windows BMP format. You might prefer a GIF format but this is not available. Go for BMP and do your batch conversion in an image processing program later.

If you have applications on your PC which are not the business standards (Word, WordPerfect etc) which are supported by PsiWin then check which formats your applications can import. The Conversion Setup dialogue to choose the nearest match.

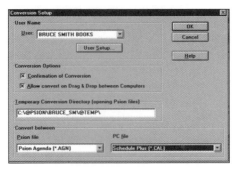

They can often cope with one of the standard formats or you may need to reduce your file to a more common denominator such as ASCII text or comma separated value (CSV) data.

If Psion File Manager can't help then you can resort to matching your file type with a Windows application. This means that when your file type is encountered, Windows knows to find the application you have specified in your match. For instance you may wish to open SCR (screen) files into Windows Paint. All you have to do is match the two in the dialogue.

From Psion	To Windows
Psion Word	Word for Windows 2.0 and 6.
	Word for Windows 6.00
	Works for Windows 3.0
	WordPerfect 5.1 DOS
	WordPerfect 5.2 DOS
	WordPerfect 6.0 for DOS
	WordPerfect 6.0 for Windows
	Ami Pro 3.0
	RTF
	Text.
Psion Sheet	Excel 5.0
	Lotus 123
	WK3
	WK1
	Quattro Pro 5.0 for Windows
	Works for Windows 3.0.
Psion Agenda	Act! 2.0
	Lotus Organizer 1.0
	Lotus Organizer 1.1
	Polaris PackRat 5.2
	Microsoft Schedule+ 1.0
Psion Data	Act! 2.0
	dBase III
	dBase IV
	Delimited text
	FoxPro 2.5
	Lotus Organizer 1.0
	Lotus Organizer 1.1
	Polaris PackRat 5.2
	Works for Windows 3.0.

Table 16.2. Psion File Manager built-in conversions.

Clip Convert

As well as the file translations available as shown in the Table, data can be transferred from a Psion application to a Windows application via the clipboard. There are clipboard translators for moving data from Psion Word to an application which supports RTF or Delimiter text, for moving data from Psion Sheet to WK1 and any application supporting Delimiter text and for moving data from Psion Data to an application accepting Delimiter text.

If, for instance, you use a Sage accounts program and you wish to transfer some names and addresses of clients to the customer list then you can cut the details from Psion Data and paste them into the Sage window. It doesn't matter that, in this case, there is no specific PsiWin translation for this data.

PsiWin does try to convert OPA files when moving them to a PC which causes

PC to Psion

Copying files from your desktop PC to your Psion Series 3 disk(s) is equally simple and involves dragging an icon from the window representing the PC's hard drive to the window representing the selected Psion disk. All this is done within Psion File Manager of course. File conversion is carried out but in reverse. For instance a Microsoft Word (.doc) file is converted to a Psion Word (.wrd) file on its way across.

There are two things which can go wrong. A file conversion can fail and this may simply be because the document can't be recognised for what it is. In this case, choose No conversion and copy the file anyway. You may have to load it and resave it later in your Psion application. Secondly, you may drop the icon in the wrong directory on your Psion Series 3 or you may (deliberately) copy lots of files into a directory with a single select/drag operation.

If this occurs, carry on with the transfer and copy the file where you need it afterwards. I use Psion File Manager to tidy up files because the drag and drop process is actually easier than using Psion System.

Running Applications

From within Psion File Manager you can double-click on a document held on your Psion Series 3 to copy it to the PC and to open it in its associated Windows program in one action.

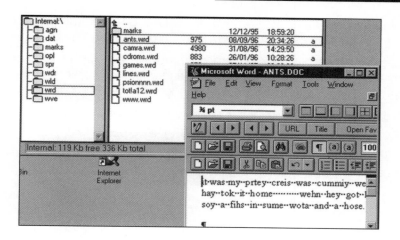

The picture above shows a WRD document in Microsoft Word, having been double-clicked on the Psion Series 3's internal drive. Any changes made within Microsoft Word must be saved to the PC hard disk and the file copied to the Psion Series 3 to keep the Psion Series 3 up to date.

Using your PC's Printer

Two utilities come as part of the PsiWin software set for printing to your desktop printer, from your Psion Series 3, using your PC as an intermediary. Print and Print Setup are the two key programs and there are full details on using these in the chapter on printing later in this book.

Data

The Data card index application on your Psion Series 3 is completely reproduced in desktop form under Windows! If you are going to use Data then first you need to transfer your Psion Series 3 file(s) containing the card information. Find the DAT directory on the Internal disk, double-click on it to open it and now drag your .dbf files across to the PC. All the files created by Data are given the .dbf suffix. You can put the files wherever you like on your desktop PC's hard drive.

Data is part of the PsiWin suite of applications. Just double-click on the icon to launch or run it from Psion File Manager under Psion/Start Psion Database.

Now you've got a fairly familiar display. It's Data, but not as we know it captain! You can use familiar hot-keys with the Windows version of Data. Just use the

Ctrl (instead of Psion) key with the hot-key. Some Data functions are represented by 'buttons' on the toolbar. Just click on them to activate.

Press the F12 key to save a card once you've entered or changed the information. If you are updating a record and make a mistake, just press the Escape key and choose Yes from the Abandon changes? dialogue.

If you don't have a file open then use the File/Open menu option.

The PC version of Data is a great place to sort out your cards. You can have more than one file open and cut and paste between them. You can sort on any label and you can merge files, killing duplicates automatically. Tidy up your data in the PC version and then export it back to your Psion Series 3.

Data has its normal two modes for searching and data entry. Press the F9 key to switch between them. The two ways of getting to a record are jumping and searching:

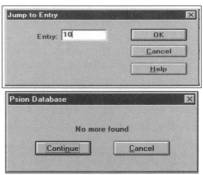

You can sort the records by field. Edit the labels to provide more and different fields for your information. Change the display through your choice of fonts and print your records. Print previewing is a luxury afforded under Windows only so make use of it.

PsiGuide begins... Printing from Psion Data (PC version)

Once you've opened your Psion Data document you can print out records which match the text you've typed into Find. Just check the Matching button.

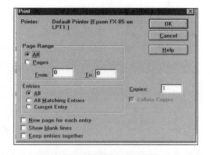

Check the results with Print preview before finally committing to paper.

PsiGuide ends

Backing up

We've mentioned the danger of losing data from your Psion Series 3 and PsiWin offers by far the best way to make a backup of information on your Psion Series 3, ready for restoration should the worst come to the worst.

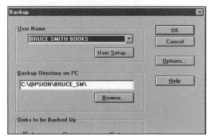

Choose Setup and Backup in Psion File Manager and adjust the settings as appropriate. Since the files which the backup process creates are useless to you in any other context, I see no reason not to leave the Backup Directory on PC as supplied. Click on Browse if you disagree and wish to specify your own spot. Your own User Name – as set up when you first used PsiWin – will appear, but can be changed so that different users can have different backups on the PC if necessary. If you don't have additional A and B disks on your Psion Series 3 then make sure these buttons are deselected.

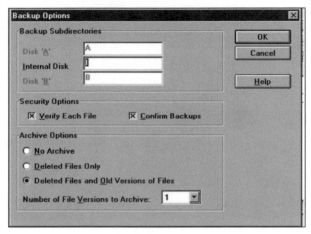

Click on Backup Options to further specify your requirements. the Backup Subdirectories can stay the same unless you are a previously a user of RCom (an earlier PC link from Psion) and wish to specify L, I and R directories to match those used by Rcom. I can't see any harm in Verify Each File and Confirm Backups.

The Archive Options settings represent three levels of 'archiving'. Archiving is making a permanent or semi-permanent copy of your files and three levels of archiving are common. Sometimes these levels are the equivalent of a time frame for archiving, such as daily, weekly and monthly. The levels represent:

1. the storage of the previous backup file.

2. files deleted on your Psion Series 3 but backed up on the PC

3. files deleted on your Psion Series 3 *and* old versions of files you've changed on your Psion Series 3 but are backed up on the PC.

It just depends how safe you like to be. If you've got plenty of space on your PC hard disk then the complete works is your best choice. It's also the default choice so you can leave it as it is. How many of these archives do you want to hang onto? The Number of File Versions to Archive offers a choice of 1, 2 or 3.

Now you've set everything up, move to the Disk menu and the Backup option and click on OK. Files being backed up are shown on screen and a status bar shows how far the copying of each file has progressed.

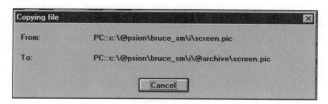

Don't get mesmerised by this display. Backing up takes place in the 'background' so you can use another program while it's going on.

Backing up automatically closes the your files on your Psion Series 3 so make sure you reopen any Agenda files to ensure that your alarms continue to operate.

Agenda and Schedule Plus

PsiWin isn't the only program which helps integrate your Psion Series 3 into the PC environment. Managing your day has become even easier thanks to a new application which works with all models of the Psion Series 3 range.

Agenda Synchronizer, developed by Time Technology Ltd, is a Windows application that allows you to update appointments on both your Psion Series 3 and the PC without losing or overwriting entries. The program links your Psion Series 3 to your PC using Microsoft Schedule Plus 1.0, via the Psion Serial Link, which is the cable part of your PsiWin package.

While you are out of the office making appointments on your Psion Series 3, in the office, secretaries and colleagues are also booking appointments on the office's networked PC diary system. All you need to do when returning to the office is to connect the Psion Series 3 to the PC, run the Agenda Synchronizer by double-clicking on its icon and it will then automatically synchronise both agendas, highlighting clashing and overlapping appointments. The whole process can run in the background and you can choose to run various reports to list clashing, overlapping and deleted appointments.

There's an incredible amount of communications options working beneath the easy to use Psion File Manager. These are available for programmers to link the Psion Series 3 to other computers systems and some of the possibilities are investigated in later chapters on communications. The programming element is beyond the scope of this book but if you are interested in this aspect of the Psion Series 3 then get in touch with the publishers for more information.

Chapter 17

Sheet Extra

 Once you've got the spreadsheet bug you'll find yourself wanting to try all sorts of things and Sheet can accommodate many of your ideas with features such as three dimensional graphs, database look-up, what-if testing with tables and a variety of functions for finance, statistics and mathematics.

If you haven't already got a spreadsheet then we can generate some random numbers. Type:

=INT(RAND*10)

into cell A1. Press ∪C to copy the contents of A1 onto the clipboard. Highlight cells A2 to A10 by using the Shift and down arrow key. Press ∪I to get a random number in each of these cells. Now we can try out some graphs.

Graphs

This is a remarkable function for a palmtop computer and it shows what the Psion Series 3 can do with its greyscale screen display. Highlight cells A1 to A10 and press the ♦ key for an instant 3D block graph display.

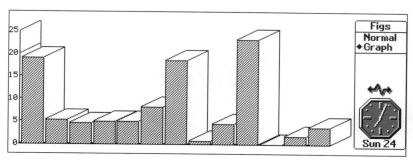

Press ∪M to have a look at the different graph formats you can display. The choice is from Bar (default), Stack-bar, Pie, Line and X./Y/Scatter. The first three of these graph types have a 3D option which you can turn on or off (Yes, No).

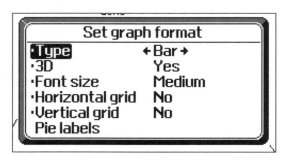

The values for the charts you can see come from the ten cells you've highlighted and you can generate graphs from any part of your spreadsheet simply by highlighting a range. The range can also be set from within Graph mode. Indeed you have a complete set of controls which you can reveal by pressing the Menu key. Choose Ranges/Set ranges and you can define six ranges for graphs A to F.

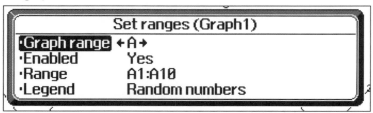

The Enabled dialogue switches the graph on or off and you can have more than one graph enabled, which lines up the graphs together.

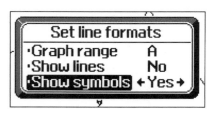

Line formats (∪L) provides control over the display for the line-based graph formats.

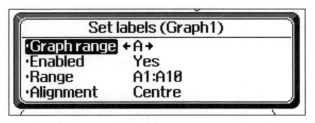

Set labels (∪B) is another range dialogue. This time you define where the labels for each value are to come from. If you leave the definition as A1:A10, the same as your graph range, you'll get the values displayed above each bar of the graph.

Back in Normal mode, use Open gap to insert a column before your figures column and add a label in front of each number so that the labels are in column A and the numbers are now in column B.

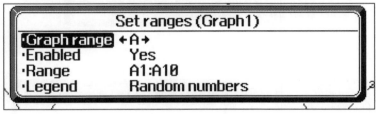

Use Set ranges to define the graph range (column B) .

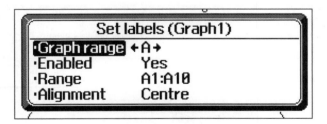

Use Set labels to define the label range (column A). The labels in column A will now appear alongside the graph of each number.

Different bars in the chart are differentiated by shading and you can display legends for each type of shading by pressing ∪V.

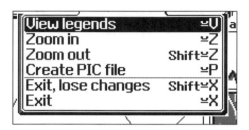

The legends come from the names you have given the range of numbers producing the graph.

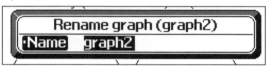

Use Rename graph (∪E) to change this legend.

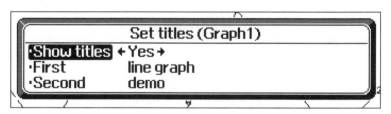

A title can be added top centre by defining two lines in Display/Titles (∪T)).

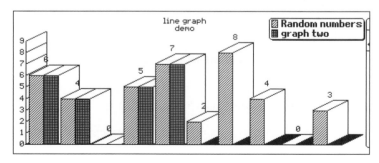

The result is a very professional graph presentation.

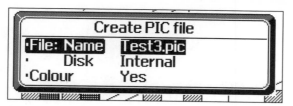

Once you've got a graph display you are happy with, it can be saved with the Sheet and you can save it separately as a .PIC file (∪P). You can even save colour information for use on a colour printer. The file when printed won't be an exact replica of the screen display. Consult your manual for the subtle differences.

You can stack a second set of figures onto a bar graph by defining another range of numbers but things can get a bit crowded on screen if you take this too far. The idea of graphs is to make numbers clearer, after all.

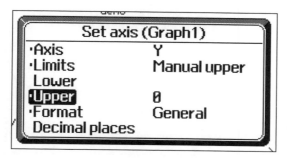

The axes of the individual graph can be defined, normally relying on the Limits field being automatically set. However you can choose Limits Manual and then fill in the Lower or Upper fields below.

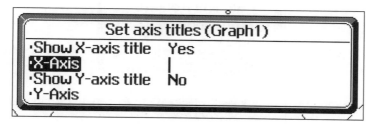

The title for each axis can also be typed in and this, once established, can be turned on and off by adjusting the Show X and Show Y axis title fields.

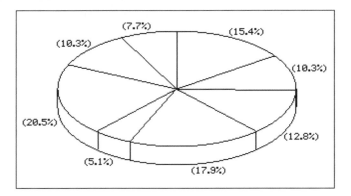

Pie charts put your figures into a pie and allocate each figure its proper portion of the slice. The numbers are automatically turned into percentages which appear as labels against the portions. The program does this for you.

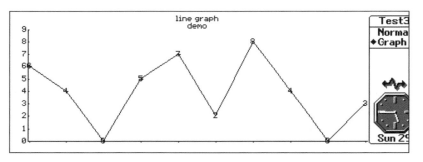

Line graphs are useful for plotting trends such as the value of the pound against the dollar or the progress of a chemical reaction.

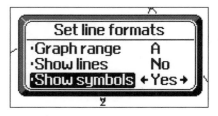

Ranges/Line formats (∪L) provides a dialogue to to control the appearance of these graphs so that you can have lines on their own or symbols on their own, both or neither.

Once you have set up a few graphs then they can be managed through Use graph (∪U), Rename graph (∪E), Delete graph (∪D) and New graph (∪N).

When you use New graph you can choose to keep the current data and change the graph style or to keep the graph style but change the data.

Functions

As well as numbers and formulae typed in by yourself, the spreadsheet program has its own built-in functions and there are plenty to choose from in Sheet. The simplest functions involve adding up columns and rows of cells. For instance, typing:

=sum(A1:A50)

will add all the values in the first 50 cells in column A because the function of 'sum' is to add up the numbers in the range defined in the brackets which follow it. Values can be obtained from most functions in this way, by preceding them with the equals sign and defining their scope in brackets.

Sheet contains functions for hundreds of purposes and it's beyond the scope of this book to give details of them all. Functions deal with numbers, formulae and other data types such as time. For instance, to store the current time and date, type '+NOW' and then format the cell as a date using View/Format/Show as/Date (⌴M).

Database

Using Sheet as an alternative database to Data is not what is intended by the provision of database features in Sheet.

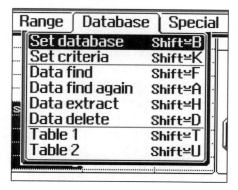

The Database feature might be better termed Lookup and it's based on the concept we've already come across on a few occasions, the range.

PsiGuide begins... Database in Sheet

Type in the small block of titles and numbers similar to those shown in the
illustration below.

B19			
A	**B**	**C**	**D**
1			
2	stock1	stock2	stock3
3	4	2	5
4	4	2	2
5	5	5	1
6	3	1	0
7			

Use the Shift and arrow keys to highlight the numbers in the range B13:D16 and
choose Database/Set database (S∪B) to make this range your current database.

stock1	stock2	stock3
4	2	5
4	2	2
5	5	1
3	1	0
crit1	crit2	crit3

Use the Shift and arrow keys to highlight the range B19:D19 as shown here.
Choose Database/Set criteria (S∪K) to make this range your current criteria.

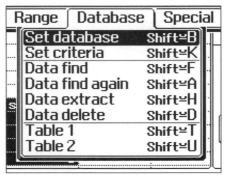

Range	Database	Special
Set database		Shift⋍B
Set criteria		Shift⋍K
Data find		Shift⋍F
Data find again		Shift⋍A
Data extract		Shift⋍H
Data delete		Shift⋍D
Table 1		Shift⋍T
Table 2		Shift⋍U

The Database tools listed in the Database menu can now be used. Data find (S∪F)
and Data find again (S∪A) use the numbers in the criteria range to find matching
data in the database range.

B	C	D
5	5	1
3	1	0
crit1	crit2	crit3
stock1	stock2	stock3

Use ∪C and ∪I to copy the row containing the field titles to another part of your sheet. Now use the Shift and arrow keys to highlight the new row of field titles and a few of the rows beneath. Leave the area highlighted and choose Data extract (S∪H). This operation takes matching records (the row is the record, the individual cell the field) and copies them into the area you highlighted previously.

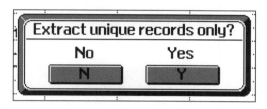

Data delete (S∪D) deletes the matching records. Edit/Undo delete can be used to bring them back if the criteria set turned out to find some records you really wanted to hang on to.

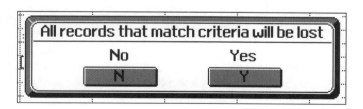

PsiGuide ends

Business Models

Spreadsheets are also commonly used for project management and for testing out 'what if' scenarios in business. Sheet can help you with this kind of work.

You can set up a sheet which contains numbers together with cells which rely on those numbers. Changes can be made to test different scenarios. In the example given here, the cell containing the retail price and the cell containing the costs can be adjusted to see the level of profits which result. Much more sophistication can be built in but this is the start point for this kind of spreadsheet.

Tables

Tables are a special 'what if' feature which Sheet provides. There are two types: Table 1 and Table 2 and these are defined simply by marking the range and choosing the menu option to make the range one of these Table types.

The first takes the values listed in a column and inputs them into a number of formulae listed in a row. Highlight the whole area, starting with the empty top left-hand cell (called the input cell) and then choose Database/Table 1 (Shift⊔T). Each cell in the body of the table is filled in with the result of the values being entered into the formulae.

To try out Table 2, enter the formula you wish to try in the top left-hand corner and list one set of values down the first column and a second set along the first row. Highlight the area and choose Table 2 (Shift⊔U). The resulting values will fill the block.

Hints and Tips

Remember that there are two ways of entering formulae. If you type in the numbers without an equal sign (=) in front then the formula will be calculated and the result entered into the cell when you press Enter. If you type an = sign and then type the formula the same result appears in the cell but the individual elements of the formula are retained and can be edited and recalculated. So remember the = sign if you want to keep the formula 'live', which is the usual requirement.

Put the cursor in cell A5 and press ⊔O, Enter to insert gap (a row) and move the information in A5 down one row. Have you spotted the problem? The contents of cell A5 moved down but the contents of the cells of B5 onwards didn't move down. When you insert or delete rows or columns, make sure that you highlight all of the row or column you wish to insert/delete before you go ahead. When the row or column next door moves to fill the gap, if you've left part of a row or column undeleted, then your layout will be disrupted. Some cells will move and others will not, damaging the 'shape' of your spreadsheet.

Use references. It's easy to put a number in but, before you know it, you've copied the cell around to lots of locations and it dawns on you, too late, that it needs to be a variable. The answer is to think through the design of your spreadsheet beforehand. Use Word or Jotter to note your requirements, where labels will appear in rows and columns and which numbers should be defined as variables.

If you include a reference in a cell to itself, a double arrow sign appears and 'recalculating' appears in top right-hand corner. Rethink your spreadsheet design to remove the clash.

Use formats. As you build up your spreadsheet you may get some funny numbers appearing in the cells which contain the results of formulae. The results are correct but the format of the numbers is not appropriate. The answer is to change the format and we'll look now at the options available.

If you are working in decimal fractions or large numbers, you'll want to change the overall format. Otherwise you may be content to go to an individual cell which is, say showing too many decimal places and choose ∪M View/Format and arrow keys through to Fixed format, with two decimal places, shown in the next line of the dialogue, being normal. Note that the top line contains Range and this is described on the second line – either a single cell or a rectangular block you've highlighted e.g.

B3:F15

The range describes the cells which will be affected by the Format change. If you want to work in a single format on the whole sheet, arrow key from Range to Default and the new format will operate until further notice. Default is for the most common format you'll need, Range is for the exceptions to this rule. Esc removes the highlight.

Chapter 18

Stylish Words

 We looked at the major features of Word in an earlier chapter and the outlining facility was brought into our discussion of Agenda, which shares it with Word. This leaves one outstanding issue as far as Word is concerned and it forms a prelude to the chapter on printing. It is the issue of style. Wordprocessing is sometimes a preliminary to printing a document so Word provides some facility to adjust the presentation of your work.

The display of styles is limited in Word but that doesn't mean you can't apply the styles, even if you can't always see them. Word overcomes this problem by displaying style tags in the margin.

Set preferences	
·Show style bar	Yes
·Text file type	Paragraph
·Show tabs	Yes
·Show spaces	Yes
·Show paragraph ends	**←Yes→**
·Show soft hyphens	Yes
·Show forced line breaks	Yes

So the first thing to do in this chapter is to choose Special/Set preferences (◡O) and choose Show style bar Yes. While we are in the dialogue, choose Yes for the Show spaces and Show paragraph ends fields to see their effect. It can be useful to have these displayed to clarify the layout of your document. They won't print out so they can't do any harm. Note that the Text file type field is set to Paragraph. This is probably the most useful but if you have a long list in Word then you may find changing this to Line will help you more quickly define styles for alternate lines.

```
BT  RE.press.facilities↵
BT  ↵
BT▶ The.new.press.viewing.gallery.requires.unimpeded
    the.complete.playing.area,.from.a.minimum.of.85%,.
    facility.↵
BT  ↵
BT  10.3+50.1*3.5=185.65↵
BT  ↵
```

Above you can see the effect of showing the special characters on screen. The BT which appears in the left-hand column before each paragraph is the style code for that paragraph (or line if you have set this option in Set preferences). The next stage is apply come different styles to different paragraphs. But there is an intermediate stage available, that of defining the styles. This takes place in the Styles menu.

Defining a Style

Styles/Style housekeeping (Shift⌣H) is your first stop and it brings up a menu of management options.

An existing style can be renamed, deleted or (re)defined. Define is also to create a new style definition from scratch if you so wish. Apply is to make a change to the text using an existing style.

To change the style of some text in your document, you highlight it and then choose Apply (⌣A). A dialogue pops up, from which you select the style definition to apply. Individual characteristics can be applied to text from the Paragraph menu and you can choose to apply to the highlighted paragraph or to all paragraphs in the document which are in the same style – another way of editing a style definition.

```
                    Define style
 Font...          Proportional 12
 ·Indents...       0.00, 0.00, 0.00
 ·Tabs...          8 tab(s) set
 ·Alignment        Justified
 ·Spacing...       12, 0, 12
 ·Outline level    9
```

Define the style through your choice of font, indents, tabs and spacing. These attributes are carried by the style wherever you apply it. You can view and change styles in the Style gallery (Shift⌣G).

```
                  Font
       ·Font          Pica
       ·Size          12
       ·Underline     Off
       Bold          ← On →
       ·Italic        Off
       Print position Normal
```

Fonts make less difference on screen than on paper so you may have to think about the characteristics of the font you are using and even try a print out with your particular printer before you can be confident of its use.

Serif fonts, like Times, are often used for the main text – or body text – of a document. Sans serif fonts, like Helvetica (or Swiss) can then be used for headings, lists etc. The fonts available to you are determined by the printer model which you have selected at the time.

Remember that you have a zoom control for displaying your document on screen. Even if you increase the size of the font, it won't change in appearance on screen. The size of the font you pick should relate to its final printout and should reflect the impact (weight) with which you wish to imbue the particular text.

The basic font style and any characteristics, such as bold or italic, are displayed and you can see which style is allocated to which paragraph by turning on Show style bar in Special/Set preferences, which causes a style code to be printed alongside. BT is Body Text, HA is heading A, HB heading B, BL a bulleted list (you have to type your own bullets!).

The character set of each font will contain more characters than can be shown on your keyboard. Press the Control key and then '2' and then 'o'. You should see 'ö'. You can generate accents by pressing the Control key together with the number keys 2 to 6, followed by the character to carry the accent. Further special characters are available by press Control and '1' followed by a keyboard character. Get a blank Word document going and give them a try.

The alignment of the text has a large bearing upon its appearance. Usually text will be Left aligned, which means that it lines up down the left margin but the line endings are 'ragged' and of different length on the right margin. Right aligning keeps things neat along the right edge and ragged on the left and is usually only used for special effect.

Justified keeps things neat on left and right, spacing the characters to make them fit the line length. This is neat but be aware that it can result in some strange spacing between words within the line. Centred is used for headings and short pieces of text which stand alone from the main document.

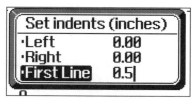

Indents have defaults so leave them alone for standard documents. The left and right indents represent the space which will appear down the side of the paper. The First line indent is for indented paragraphs. Secretarial style calls for block paragraphs so this should be set to 0.00 in this case.

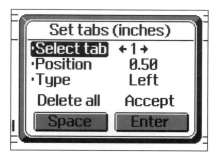

Tabulation is a bit of mystery to typists everywhere and Word is not the most flexible of applications in this respect. There are eight points across the 'page'

at which tab stops can be placed. Pressing the Tab key will then move the cursor to these points in turn.

The usefulness of tabs is that you can place a piece of text at a tab stop so that it is a fixed distance away from another piece of text at another tab stop. Use the tab key to separate text in this way instead of typing lots of spaces. If you wish to change the distance between two tab stops you can return to the Set tabs dialogue to reposition one the of the tab stops, closer or further away as needs be. When you make this change, all the text positioned at this tab stop will change position consistently, keeping your neat 'tabbed' format. Different paragraphs can have different tab stop positions.

In the dialogue you need to define each tab stop in turn. It can help to have a piece of paper and a ruler to hand. Just mark the paper where you want the text to appear and measure from the left-hand margin. Enter the measurements into your dialogue and press Enter to accept them. You will always need to reposition tabs to reflect the length of text you are positioning. Don't be afraid to define a tab stop as Centre or Right. Right tab stops are necessary to line up numbers correctly, with units under units, tens under tens and so on.

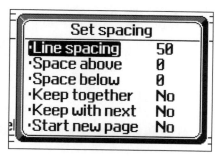

Spacing is a subtle part of text formatting which will probably need little adjustment from the default supplied. Line spacing can be increased to help readability. Space above and below can be adjusted for the tops and bottoms of paragraphs which contain tables or lists. Keep together and Keep with control where word and paragraph breaks can occur.

These same attributes can be applied directly to paragraphs – without the use of styles – through the Paragraphs menu. However defining styles beforehand is the most efficient way to impose style on your document. If you consistently apply the styles you've defined for headings, subheadings, body text, lists, tables etc then you can very quickly ring the changes.

This is done by tweaking the style definition, not by directly applying attributes to the text. By changing the style definition you make the change(s) in the whole document. As a document increases in size, this saves a lot of time and ensures the consistency mentioned above.

Emphasis

A level below the style is the emphasis, which can be applied to text which is already in a certain style. You define these additional attributes in Emphasis housekeeping (Shift∪K) and view them in Emphasis gallery (Shift∪E). It's more common to apply attributes such as bold and italic directly to the text but, as with style definitions, creating an emphasis definition can pay dividends when wholesale changes are required.

To quickly apply an emphasis, press the Control key and type 'BB' for bold, 'II' for italic, 'UU' for underline, SS for subscript, EE for superscript and NN for normal.

Sharing Styles

You can move a style or emphasis definition over to another document by pressing ∪C to copy a highlighted piece of the text which contains the style definition, moving to the System screen, pressing Shift and Enter over another (target) document and then pressing ∪B to bring the text in. If the style definition names clash then you'll need to delete or rename in the target document.

Once you have set up styles and emphases for a particular type of document, why not save it as a template ready to re-use over and over again. Over time you will build up a portfolio of templates to cover your everyday needs.

When you've put so much work into the appearance of your document it sometimes comes as a shock that you can't take much of it with you when you transfer the text to another wordprocessor on your desktop PC or need to send it to a colleague. RTF to the rescue! You can choose to save your document in Rich Text Format (RTF) from the Save as dialogue in Word. This file will then be read by another wordprocessor which will interpret the style information as best it can, often quite a close copy of the original. So your hard work in Word can result in stylish documents wherever they may go!

Chapter 19

··

Printing
Press

The key to using a printer with the Psion Series 3 is the availability of a suitable printer 'model' (sometimes called 'driver'). This will be one of the Psion printer models provided with the Psion Series 3 or it could be an equivalent supplied by a third party to support one of the more unusual printers. You can also print via your desktop PC using PsiWin. All this, and more on printers, is covered in this chapter.

Printing is no straightforward matter. Text and pictures are held as computer data in memory and displayed by different methods on different devices such as the Psion Series 3 screen, a fax machine, a pager, or a printer.

Printing Directly

The Psion Series 3 can link to a printer via the serial link or via a serial to parallel adapter. Most printers have parallel ports designed for connection to desktop computers so the Psion Series 3 needs an intermediate stage which adapts the serial data to the parallel port, and this is provided by the Psion 'parallel link'. The very latest printers have infrared connections which the Psion Series 3c and Siena can 'talk to' by sending their data via their infrared capability. Just press the send button and you are away. A suitable printer is described in the appendix on hardware and peripherals.

Printing via a PC

You've already come across PsiWin in an earlier chapter so, if you've read that, you are already ahead of the game because it can play an important role in using a remote printer attached to a PC. This has two benefits: additional features of the printer become available; you only need to buy one printer for desktop and palmtop.

Printer Types

The Psion Series 3 can print to a portable printer or a desktop printer. Some suitable portables are described in the Products appendix at the end of this book. In this chapter I'll complete the picture with a round-up of printer technologies and what you can expect to achieve from the different methods of printing available to you.

There is a wide and varied range of printer types which are classified by the way in which they perform the process of printing. The more popular methods are detailed briefly below.

Daisywheel

The grand old daisywheel has a typewriter action which results in perfectly formed characters if all you need is A to Z and 0 to 9. If you see one secondhand then it may have serial port so it's ready to go!

Thermal

The thermal printer has come back into its own for portable printers and for colour reproduction. You'll struggle to drive a colour thermal, even via a PC, but see the Products appendix for some portable printers which use this technology.

Inkjet/Bubblejet

The inkjet, and near relation, the bubblejet, squirt ink and have won popular acclaim over the last few years for producing 'laser' quality at near dot-matrix prices. The Canon Bubblejet, Hewlett Packard Deskjet and Epson Stylus are common brands. The Canon Bubblejet for example has 48 jets which give a resolution of 360 dots per inch (dpi), a more detailed printout than most laser printers can achieve. There are models for Canon BJ (Bubblejet) and HP (Hewlett Packard) Deskjet already built into your Psion Series 3.

Inkjet printing is also the key to the best colour printing on a budget. The Hewlett Packard DeskjetC is supported by a built-in printer model.

Dot Matrix

Dot matrix printers are the most successful breed of printers, partly because they are cheap to purchase and cheap to run, partly because they reproduce both text and graphics to an acceptable quality. Dot matrix printers fall into the two main categories of 9-pin and 24-pin, the latter offering better quality and speed in most cases. There are some 18-pin and 48-pin printers.

Dot matrix printers come in different carriage (paper) widths, can accommodate sheet feeders (like a photocopier) for business stationery and can be fitted with a mechanism to print in colour via four different colour ribbons. The versatility of the dot matrix is its strong point. Nor have the possibilities been exhausted as new methods of describing graphical displays to the printer mechanism are invented and incorporated into computer software.

The latest dot matrix printers have colour printing mechanisms as standard. These print through a multicoloured ribbon under software control. The printer model detects which colour is being sent and sends the appropriate code to move the ribbon into position. 24-pin dot matrix colour printouts are very impressive, though a little slow and noisy. The Epson RX and LQ models built into the Psion Series 3 support most of the features of dot-matrix printers.

Laser

The classic office laser printer is based on the Hewlett Packard Laserjet standard and you'll find appropriate models in the Psion Series 3. Lasers come with trays which hold single sheets and their print quality is usually 300 dots per inch or 600 dots per inch.. Running costs vary greatly and may be too much for home use.

PostScript

PostScript is a page description language. You will be more used to a program displaying text and graphics on your screen and your screen is a pattern of dots turned on and off by the program. Well PostScript is a program which creates the dot pattern inside a printer, which is then transferred to paper for us to view it. Normal printing operations don't use PostScript to anywhere near its full extent. It comes into its own when used by applications for desktop publishing and complex drawing.

The Psion Series 3 however does include two relevant models, one for general PostScript and one for the Apple Laserwriter, a popular PostScript printer, usually attached to a Macintosh.

It is useful to be able to send the PostScript output to a file on a disk as opposed to sending it directly to the printer. This file, which is a computer program, can be sent to the printer at any stage and can also be copied to other computers such as PCs or Apple Macintoshes which are more likely to have a PostScript printer attached.

If professional printing is required, typically for flyers, newsletters, brochures etc created in a Desktop Publishing program, then imagesetting is the intermediate stage. You send your file to an imagesetting bureau and they run it through their typesetter. The typesetter usually outputs either a positive image on photographic paper (bromide) or a negative image on transparent film. If colour is involved then the bureau will separate the colours and output four films. The bromide or film (depending on what your printer requires) is then used to create the plates which go on the printing machinery.

New Printer Models

If there is no printer model for your printer available (see below on Print setup) then you'll need to go looking! Try the manufacturer of the printer, Psion and your friendly Shareware library. If you are connected, try searching the libraries in the CompuServe palmtop forums and on other related Internet sites.

Once you've found your model you'll probably need to install it from your desktop PC. Copy it over via PsiWin, or similar Psion link, into the WDR directory on the internal disk.

Printer Control

In the System screen, choose Control/Printer (∪Y) and a Printer configuration dialogue appears. This same dialogue can be accessed via the Print setup menu of the Psion applications.

```
┌──────────────────────────────────────────────┐
│           Printer configuration               │
├──────────────────────────────────────────────┤
│ ·Printer device            Serial             │
│ ·Serial characteristics ...  19200...         │
│ ·Serial handshaking ...    Xon/xoff On...     │
│  File: Name                                   │
│        Disk                                   │
├──────────────────────────────────────────────┤
│ Units                     ← Centimetres →     │
│ ·Print preview...          4 pages, Margins on│
└──────────────────────────────────────────────┘
```

When Printer device is set to Parallel then the rest of the top portion of the dialogue is not required. When it is set to Serial, the default settings for Serial characteristics and Serial handshaking should normally be retained. If you do have problems with a serial printer then check out the chapter in this book on Comms before trying any new settings.

The third option for Printer device is File. This send the document you are printing, together with any codes needed by the particular printer model you are using, to a file on your Psion internal disk. The filename and its location can be specified in this dialogue if required.

The bottom portion of this dialogue sets the units – Inches or Centimetres – in which page sizes and so on will be expressed. Press Tab over the Print preview option to view the sub-dialogue and choose the number of pages (1 to 4 and facing) to display in the on-screen preview which is available from the print dialogues in the applications. You can also choose whether to have the margin on or off. Personally the more preview pages the better but it does depend on your document layout so think through what you need to see before printing for real.

Printing from Applications

Most of your printing will be done from within an application. Each Psion application prints through the same printer model but of course the document you are printing is different and may require some adjustments to be made. For instance, if you are printing from Sheet then you may wish to print in landscape format, with the top of your document printed along the long edge of the paper. In this way you can get more on each piece of paper. You'll have noticed that, although the computer screen is usually wider than it is deep, printer paper is usually deeper than it is wide!

Print setup	
·Page size...	A4
·Margins...	1.25, 1.25, 1.25, 1.25
·Header...	
·Footer...	%P
·Paging control...	1, No, 1,2,3
·Printer model...	Psion Print
·Printer device...	Serial

The place for this kind of adjustment is Special/Print setup (∪Y). The dialogue is split into two. The top gives you a chance to match the settings of the document with those of the paper you are using.

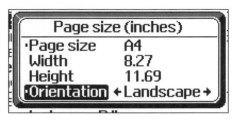

Press Tab over Page size to configure the size by name. The measurements below may change to reflect these and can be used to check whether your paper is the right size. The Orientation field has portrait and landscape settings.

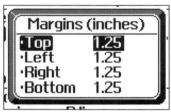

Margins are the spaces which appear around your text on the piece of paper and the default settings are usually suitable. Remember that setting a larger margin takes away from the amount of paper left for the text. In other words the block of text will be narrower when printed.

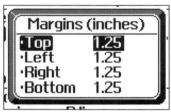

Back in the main dialogue, a Header field can be completed. This is the place to put the project or document title which you wish to have repeated on each page of the printout.

```
            Enter footer details (inches)
·Text              page %P
·Alignment         Centred
On first page     ← Yes →
·Font...            Courier New 12
·Vertical offset   0.50
```

The Footer field contains the page number by default (%P) but you can replace this or add to it with your own text. You may wish to type %P into the Header to have the page number printed at the top of the page. Use %D for date, %T for time, % for filename and %% for the % character.

```
              Paging control
·Number for first page      11
·Allow widows/orphans       No
Page number style       ← i,ii,iii →
```

The Page control field provides a Paging control dialogue which lets you renumber you first page. If you have a document in two parts in two different files then you will wish to renumber the first page of the second file to that following the last page of the first file. Allow widows/orphans does a check on your text for you. If a single line of text from a paragraph is going to print over on the next page or only a single line will fit on the bottom of a page then this check will prevent it by pushing another line over the page or splitting the page at the paragraph. This neatens up your printouts no end.

The bottom part of this dialogue is concerned with the printer model and any available model can be selected. The default is taken from the Printer Configuration dialogue in the System screen and if your printer hasn't changed, you don't need to change it here.

```
                 Set printer
Select printer  ← Psion Print →
Default font...    Courier New 12
```

The printer device can also be adjusted, for instance to send data to a print file. Once again, the default is taken from the Printer Configuration dialogue in the System screen.

Print Preview

The Special/Print preview option (∪*) provides control on an individual application basis.

Data

In Data Special/Print preview (∪*) is important because it provides control over what gets printed where. You can choose No for New page for each entry which is often wasteful of paper. In the Entries field you can choose between All, Matching and Current.

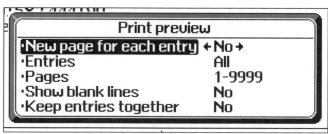

Matching is very handing because it only prints out those records which match the Find text you have entered. Show blank lines No also saves on paper and Keep entries together Yes/No is a matter of personal preference. The Print (∪P) option offers some of this control as well.

Word

Print preview (∪*) in Word provides familiar control over pages and copies – which pages and how many copies of each.

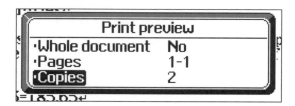

The Print (∪P) option provides identical control. If you wish to print a section of your document you'll have to copy the section, create a new document and insert the copied text into it before printing from this new document.

Sheet

In Sheet you can select a range of cells and set them as the Print range (ShiftꞯR).

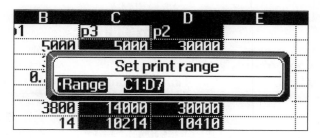

In both Print preview (ꞯ*) and Print (ꞯP) you can select between printing this previously defined print range or the whole worksheet.

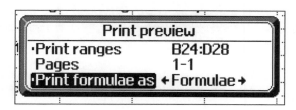

If more than one page is involved you can specify the range to print and you can print out cell contents as formulae to help you 'debug' your worksheet.

Agenda

The print options are considerable in Print (ꞯP) and Print Preview (ꞯ*) in Agenda. The Range of entries field can be chosen from:

Whole Agenda

From today	Until today
This week	Last week
This month	Last month
This year	Last year

Print	
·Range of entries	From today
·Start date	22/01/1997
End date	02/10/**1998**
·Repeat entries	Not shown
·Crossed out entries	Yes
·Entry types...	Timed,Untimed,Annivs,To-dos

Additional control comes from the Start date and End date fields to restrict the range to print. The second part of the dialogue is handy because you often don't want to print out all the repeating entries, nor the crossed out entries.

Entry types to print	
Timed entries	←Yes→
·Untimed entries	Yes
·Anniversaries	Yes
·To-dos	Yes

Finally press Tab over the Entry types field to choose Yes/No for Timed entries, Untimed entries, Anniversaries and To-dos.

Applications can also establish the style and content of a printed document when you can't display the equivalent on screen. For instance, printing an Agenda list replicates the priorities set in Agenda, listed by date or priority for instance. Here's a sample printout:

<u>projectX</u>

[1]   hire AV equipment

[2]   order stationary

[1]   call conference room

[1]   remember mums birthday card (25/12/96)

<u>ProjectY</u>

[9]   target1 (2/12/96)

[9]   target2 (4/12/96)

[9]   target3 (8/12/96)

<u>To-do list</u>

etc…

Preview Control

When viewing a print preview, press Menu to bring up the Preview menu.

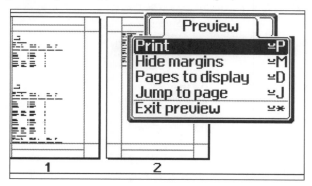

This offers immediate control over some of the options we've already covered, such as margins.

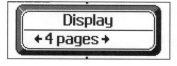

You can also reconfigure the number of pages to display and jump to a particular page. When you are happy with everything, you can choose Print.

Printing Via Your PC

Psion Print, which comes as part of the PsiWin software, is a great way of printing from your Psion Series 3 to the printer attached to your PC. This is an economical way of getting quality output directly from your Psion Series 3 without having to buy the top notch portable printers.

If you don't have to print out in the field then bring your files on home to give them a proper route to paper.

Psion Print can simply be called up from Psion File Manager or you can launch it on its own. It needs a bit of setting up before you can use it so it's time for a PsiGuide.

PsiGuide begins... Printing with Psion Print

Your Psion Series 3 may not know about the printer attached to your PC so the first thing to do is to copy (download) the correct printer model to your Psion Series 3.

You can check which printer you are using by clicking on your Printers folder in Windows. It's the default printer which your Psion Series 3 will use to print.

Now click on the Psion Print Setup icon, which is in the Psion program group. You can reach this from the Start/Programs menu in Windows 95.

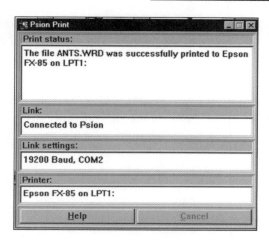

Windows makes use of TrueType fonts when it prints so your Psion Series 3 also needs to know about these. Click on Install fonts and choose those you wish to install by clicking on their names in the left-hand list of Available fonts. The fonts you've selected appear in the right-hand window Selected fonts.

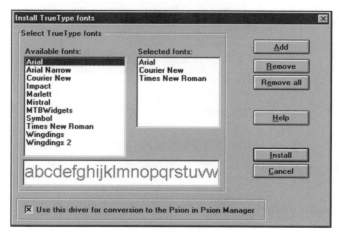

Click on Install to send the font and printer definition information to your Psion Series 3. In fact Times New Roman, Arial and Courier New are automatically copied when you run Psion Manager. If you have the space then move the other fonts you like the look of, except Script or Symbol.

Click on the Printer button, choose one of the listed printers – those available from Windows (see above). Click on OK. Click on the close button of the Psion Print Setup window.

Now from Word (or Sheet or other Psion application) you can print your document on the printer attached to your desktop PC. Choose Print setup from the Special menu. Move to the Printer model field and press Tab. In the Set printer dialogue, use the arrow keys to get Psion Print in the Select printer field.

Run Psion Print by clicking on its icon on your PC screen or by choosing Psion/Start Psion Print from Psion File Manager. Select Special/Print and press Enter to confirm the details which appear.

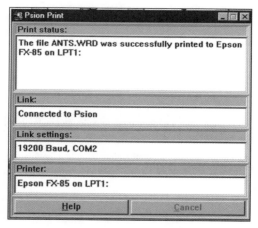

The Print progress window shows you what's going on. You can cancel printing from here. Exit the Psion Print window when you've finished your printing session.

PsiGuide ends

Chapter 20

System Setup

 You can change your Psion Series 3's settings to suit your own requirements. Let's open the bonnet and get our hands dirty! The System screen has its own set of menus. The first couple, File and Disk, provide access to the filing system (see Chapter 14). The third menu tree is Apps and it controls the display and operation of applications. The built-in applications will rarely give you trouble and you may never dream of, for instance, removing one from the System screen. But you can if you want.

Remove (∪/) – sounds dangerous doesn't it – pops up a Yes/no dialogue asking if you want to remove the application you have highlighted in the System screen. Now this won't delete the program so that you can never use it again but it will remove the application's icon from the System screen.

A likely candidate for removal form your initial System screen is Program if you don't do any programming. Move to the Program icon with the arrow keys and press ∪/ and Y. The icon disappears.

Now move to Install standard (∪J) and a dialogue will offer you the chance to put the Program icon back. This is also how you can move your icons about, by removing them and then reinstalling them and choosing their new position.

Use Install (∪I) when you wish to place an application which isn't built in on to the System screen. This could be a program you've copied from a PC via PsiWin or it could be a program you've purchased on a SSD.

Choose the disk from which to install the application in the dialogue and then choose the file name.

Meltdown

Exit application (Shift⏷K) and Exit all applications (Shift⏷A) are useful if you want to close down an application from the System screen, often to save memory before using another application. The open applications are those shown in bold type on your System screen. You can also close down an open application by highlighting the open file and pressing the Delete key.

In this section of the menu is the delightfully named Kill application. This is your last resort in case the application does something strange or 'hangs', 'freezes' or otherwise lets you down.

If you get an error message from your Psion then there's a long way to go before you need to panic! The message usually takes a form similar to this:

> **Error**
> **AGENDA.$.09**
> **Process exited**
> **Exit number 73**
> **Continue**
> **ESC**

Here the program Agenda has 'crashed', broken down temporarily and is no longer available to work in. You'll need to start it up again. For the moment you are asked to press ESC to leave the error message and return to the System screen. This message doesn't necessarily mean that you've lost any information you've entered however.

When you re-open your Agenda file you may find that the program anticipated the 'crash' and that your data is intact. A 'fatal' error is rare but I've tried to delete a timed entry in Agenda and been faced with the horror:

> **TIME.$.06**
> **Process exited**
> **Exit number 60**
> **Continue**
> **ESC**

and pressed Escape and nothing happened. The keyboard didn't respond and I thought I'd got an ex Series 3. Well, I turned of for a while to collect my thoughts and to calm down. Next, on turning on, I pressed the System icon and it worked. However on returning to Agenda, nothing except a black square floating on the screen! I closed everything down and freed up memory as best I could but nothing. This is where Kill application comes in. If you have potentially lost data, what can you do? Backup your files as best you can and if Kill application doesn't work, you can reset your Series 3 by poking something into the tiny hole just above the ON key. This is not the end of the world either because, in my experience, data is retained. A parting piece of advice: where possible, be a methodical troubleshooter!

Assign

The last tool in this group is Assign button (∪A). This isn't of immediate use when you are using the standard programs which you have on your System Screen but if you purchase, or perhaps write your own, program then you may want to be able to start up in that program by pressing one of the 'buttons' (the icons) on the front panel of the Psion Series 3. Aren't they already used for the main programs? Yes, the buttons on the front of the Psion Series 3 are reserved for standard apps but, by pressing the Control key and one of these buttons, it's possible to launch into any program as long as you've assigned the button.

Let's use the Record program as an example. The Record icon doesn't appear amongst the buttons on the front of your Psion Series 3 so it needs to be assigned to one of the Control key/button combinations.

Move to Record with the arrow keys and press ∪A. The dialogue title bar should display 'Assign button to "Record"'. If you are assigning a button to a different program then its name will appear between the quote marks. The first combination offered is Control+Data. The Data icon is the first button available left to right. Use the arrow keys to change this setting. The Modifier field below has two settings: Control and None. A modifier is a key which modifies the action of another key, or button. We are using the Control key to modify the actions of the buttons. If you choose None then you are assigning an action to the button alone.

Audio

The next System menu to provide control over your Psion Series 3 is appropriately called Control. Control/sound (∪S) has four options, the first of which, All sound, just turns sound On or Off. Sound plays a surprisingly important part in the use of the Psion Series 3 so I recommend you leave it on. In which case there are three further options.

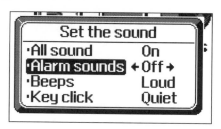

Alarm sounds is another On/off choice and this should positively be left on if alarms are to be of use. Sometimes you hesitate for a moment when some strange noise emanates from your bag or pocket but, embarrassment over, you get the important reminder you needed from your Psion Series 3 alarm.

Beeps can be set Loud, Quiet, or Off. Beeps occur when there's and error or the System wishes to alert you to something and hence you need to hear them. If you carry the Psion Series 3 around in cars and trains, like me, then you'll need to set to Loud.

Key click is a contentious one. Should it be Loud, Quiet or Off? I've never used keyclick on a desktop computer but that's because the keys are big enough to let you know if they've ben pressed or not. Keyclick can give you an audio alert of the fact that a key hasn't been properly depressed by not making a noise. I therefore think this has a use but keep an open mind on the volume. Constant key-clicking can annoy other passengers, unless they are on their mobile phone or listening to their Walkman at the time!

A quick press (∪S) to turn sound on and off is useful if you wish to suppress the audio element of an alarm when you really don't want to disturb fellow travellers or disrupt a meeting.

Print Power

Printer (∪Y) brings up a formidable-looking Printer configuration dialogue. Leave it well alone is my advice! Seriously, unless you've got a printer, do just that: nothing. If you do have a printer then there's a complete chapter on the subject to work through (Chapter 19). If you're curious at this stage, you'll discover that you can print to a serial or parallel printer – with the right connections which are not provided with your Psion Series 3 – or you can print to a file. The latter technique means you needn't have a printer for the Psion Series 3 at all but can transfer your files onto a desktop computer. It's also possible – with PsiWin and other third party software – to print via a PC without leaving your own wordprocessor.

```
                 Printer configuration
·Printer device          Serial
·Serial characteristics ...  19200...
·Serial handshaking ...   Xon/xoff On...
 File: Name
      Disk
 Units                    ← Centimetres →
·Print preview...         4 pages, Margins on
```

The bottom section of the printer control dialogue is worth a brief look now. The Units option is for working in inches or centimetres and it's a difficult one. These days I plump for Euro measurements although the influence of USA-based software is keeping the inch in business.

On Print preview, hit Tab for a sub-dialogue called Preview settings. The Display can be one, two, three, four or facing pages. This effects the print preview functions of Word, Data, Sheet and Agenda.

A four page preview fits neatly across the screen and so can't think of a reason not to select this. In Word facing pages might be handy if you are working in two page chunks for a flyer or similar output.

Other Controls

Auto switch off we've used and it is important for the preservation of your battery life.

```
              Set auto switch off
 Auto switch off  ← Yes →
·Switch off time    00:05:00
```

Batteries are the bane of all portable computer users' lives but the Psion Series 3 keeps you computing when you need to, warns you like mad when power is getting low, and you are very unlikely to lose any information so there's no need to panic. Always play safe of course but, on the other hand, don't worry too much if you are far from base and need to keep on going a bit when the warning messages are flashing up.

Lots of other electrically powered items can use the standard 1.5V batteries which the Psion Series 3 uses so keep your Psion Series 3 well provided and use the old Psion Series 3 batteries for things like children's remote control cars, your camera flash and kitchen scales!

I'm grateful to a letter from John Linn in New York, USA, which appeared in Palmtop magazine for the information that rechargeable alkaline batteries called 'Ray-O-Vac Renewals' cost just a bit more than long-life batteries but have a good shelf life and can be charged a few dozen times. A charger costs around $10. Average use on a set is 40 hours plus.

The CR1620 backup batteries are available in Halfords where they are aimed at users of car alarms and remote controls.

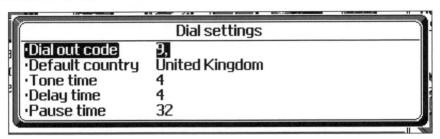

Dialling (Shift⌣D) brings up the Dial settings dialogue. Unless you are having trouble then leave well alone and note the original settings if you are going to have a meddle.

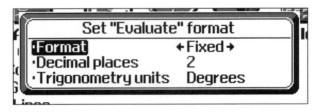

Evaluate format (Shift⌣E) offers control over the number format which the evaluate function will produce when used in Word, Data etc. Four formats are offered and these are explained in detail in Chapter 11.

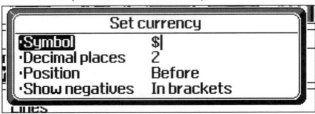

Number separators and Currency format are important for a jet-setting palmtop like the Series 3. Use Tab to get the detailed dialogues and try to match the two according to the conventions of the country or profession concerned.

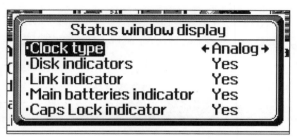

The Status window (Shift∪W) controls what appears in the System screen and is mainly cosmetic. The Special menu contains some more substantial options, firstly in Set preferences (∪O). In this dialogue you choose when to update the lists which appear under the applications icons.

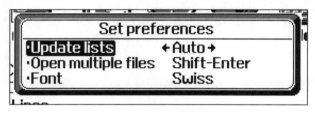

Open multiple files sets the key press to open a second and subsequent files in one application. Normally pressing Enter over a file will open only that file. If a file is already open then it will be closed. The new open file will progress to the top of the file list and will be displayed in bold. Pressing Shift and Enter over a file however will open it as a second open file. You can then switch between these files via the System screen.

The choice of Font is between Swiss, default and Sans Serif, and Times, Serif.

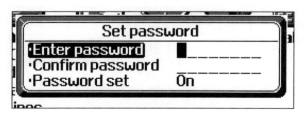

Password (⊍W) protects your Series 3 from prying eyes. But do you need it? If you genuinely require protection then take precautions to keep your password from others but make sure you can remember it when you need to. You can choose your password and then set it Off in the dialogue if you wish to turn it on and off to suit.

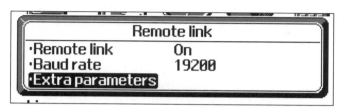

Remote link (⊍L) comes into play when you connect your Series 3 via the serial port. See the chapters on PsiWin and Comms.

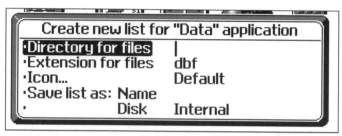

Create new list (⊍E) takes you through a file creation dialogue. If you are creating a list of spreadsheet files then highlight a spreadsheet file before pressing ⊍E. The default directory is then determined as SPR. Any other directory you specify here will be a subdirectory of SPR. On creation, a new icon with a copied list appears on the System screen. The files can be deleted like any other and you can use Apps/Remove (⊍/) to get rid of it again.

Create new group (⊍G) brings together more than one list into a single icon. The applications in the group are listed beneath the icon. When you've used Install (your own lists or new applications) or Install standard to put in-built applications into the group, you can then remove the original icons from the System screen to have a tidy up.

PsiGuide begins... Grouping applications

Make sure you are in the System screen. Highlight the icon where you want to create the new group. The icon will be inserted to the left of this position.

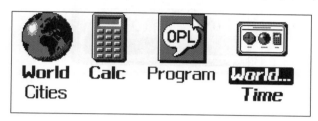

Press ∪G and give your new group a name before pressing Enter. The group icon appears in your System screen. Note that the World icon remains even though World is also now in the new group. Use Remove on World to tidy up the display.

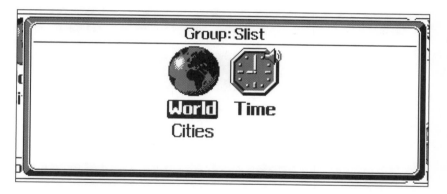

Highlight the name beneath the group icon and press Space.

Press ⌴J and choose the built-in applications you wish to group. You'll have to press ⌴J for each application and make sure that you've pressed Space beforehand otherwise it won't work. Time and World are always good candidates for grouping.

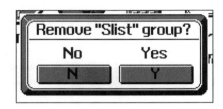

You can remove the new group at any time and restore the individual applications using Install standard.

PsiGuide ends

Chapter 21

Sonic Boon

Record sounds for use in alarm calls and save voice memos for your to-do lists and diary entries. Talking to your Psion Series 3 beats talking to yourself!

Apart from the fun of recording and making noises with your Psion Series 3, sound can play a practical role in time management functions and sometimes recording a brief memo can be easier than having to use the keyboard. It's all made possible by the Record program and this chapter explains how to use it.

Choose Record from the System screen and you are presented with a statement at the top along the lines of

     Record   2.0 sec   16 Kbyte

and below, three 'buttons'

     Tab   Space   Enter

If you've just begun, only the first option is of interest so let's record new. What is about to happen? The Psion Series 3 can store information in its memory. We've seen various ways that it does this and we've come across different formats which it gives information stored in memory. Well, here's a new kind of format for a new kind of information. The format is called WAV and the information is digital sound.

Digital Sound

Unless you're one of these hi-fi purists – and nothing wrong with that – you've probably got a CD player in your home somewhere. You may even be listening on a portable Walkman type as you read this, heaven forfend! Compact Disc did away with 'grooves' on the old LPs and introduced us to the idea of holding music as bits and bytes etched into the surface, as ups and downs, of a CD. Your CD player has sufficient computer processing power to interpret the bits and bytes back into electrical currents which eventually generate the sounds you hear via your amplifier and speakers.

The reason I'm turning this chapter into What Hi-fi? is to explain that sound can be stored digitally. The Psion Series 3 stores its bits and bytes in memory. And where does the Psion Series 3 get the sounds to store? From the Record application. Record 'grabs' bits and bytes form a chip in the Psion Series 3 called an analogue to digital converter (ADC). The chip's sole purpose is to interpret sounds as bits and bytes, and vice versa. So it's also a digital to analogue converter (DAC).

Recording a Sound

To record a sound you are going to look foolish in front of your friends or neighbours by talking into your computer. Alternatively you can put the Psion Series 3 up against your radio or sound your card horn! Your Psion Series 3 contains a microphone which is situated in the bottom right-hand corner of the underside of the unit, in front of the 'B' slot which holds the backup batter.

The microphone converts you sound into electrical signals and these are converted into bits and bytes through a technique called 'sampling' – hence the term for this whole process is 'sound sampling' and the sound which is stored in digital form is know in shorthand as a 'sample'.

A 'sample' on the Psion Series 3 is stored as a sequence of bits and bytes which the Record application can recognise and interpret as sounds. The filename of the sample is given a WAV extension to show that it's a sound sample. WAV is also the extension used on PCs for sound samples but the two formats are not the same even though they have a name in common. You can't use Psion WAV samples on a PC and vice versa. Conversion programs are available however. See the chapter on PsiWin.

High quality sound samples are the basis of electronic keyboards and techno and rave music is crammed full of samples. both of instruments and other sounds, and of whole extracts form other songs. This we can't achieve on the Psion Series 3. Psion's SoundStudio application, available as standard on the Series 3c, can make things more aurally interesting, as we will investigate later.

Even without SoundStudio, the Record application does provide one vital techno technique – the loop. It's designed for a repeating alarm but it's perfectly possible to design something which will get 'em dancing – if only it could be heard at more than two feet!

Sound Sampling

In the meantime, now you know how it works, you can get back to the Record application, waiting patiently for you to press the Tab key to sample sound.

Press Tab and you get a dialogue confirming your wish to 'Record to new file' under the name 'Record01' on the 'Internal' disk, with a 'Maximum duration (sec)' of 2.0 seconds. The 2.0 is highlighted so you can immediately type in a new figure here if you wish.

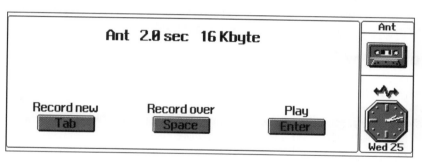

The message

Record01   2.0 sec   16 Kbyte

should now make sense. The sound will be stored under the name 'Record01', will be two seconds long and will take up 16K of memory storage space. Try one second (9K) and three seconds (24K) to see how long you get. In the dialogue use the arrow keys to move to the 'File: Name field' and change it to something meaningful eg horn, shout, dog. You'll soon forget which sound you put under Record01.

Press Enter to confirm the details and prepare to sample! All it takes now is a press of the Space bar.

When you press Space your Psion Series 3 starts recording – it doesn't wait for you to start making a noise so be ready or the first part of your sample will be wasted. You may not be able to edit the sample later so it's best to get it right when recording.

A bar, representing the total sample time, is displayed and this fills up from left to right to give you a visual prompt to the time taken. If you want to abandon the sample, press Esc at any time, even in the middle of recording. In the latter case the half-finished sample is saved under the filename given.

Working with Sounds

If you are recording a number of sounds in one session then it's often best to save under the name Record01 and let the program automatically number the next sound Record02, Record03 etc. When you've finished, you can go to the System screen to rename the files and delete any that didn't work out. You won't be able to delete any active Record file.

Alternatively, if you rehearse a sample and it doesn't sound OK when you press Enter to hear it, you can press Space to 'Record over' the last effort. The sample is saved under the same filename and doesn't take up any more memory. You can also edit the filename in the dialogue box back to the previous name and confirm that you wish to overwrite the previously saved file.

Free memory is important to your Psion Series 3's operation so it's worth experimenting with the maximum duration setting to get it just the right size for the duration of your sample. If the sample is 'clipped' at the end then you need a bit more time. If the bar is still filling up when you've already finished your sound(s) then you can cut back a bit. You can adjust in 100ths of a second, eg 0.05 sec, so you can fine tune the duration!

Record has a few menu items to take account of. New file is the equivalent of pressing Tab, prompting for file and sound sample details. Open file lets you open a previous sample to play it back and to Record over if you're not happy with it.

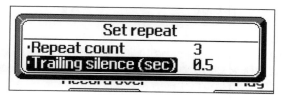

Set repeat is the nearest to rave disc jockey you can get with the Psion Series 3! In the dialogue you can adjust the number of repeats – up to 1000 – and you can insert a 'rest' between each repeat of the sample. The rest, termed 'Trailing silence (sec)' can be up to 1000 seconds long.

When you press Enter the nature of the sound sample is changed slightly and some new information displayed on screen. What Record does is to take your request for, say, five repeats with three second intervals, and it stores this information with the sound sample. It doesn't nee to replicate the sound sample five times, only to tell the Psion Series 3 application, eg Alarm, that this sample is to be repeated as requested. After completing these settings you'll see something like this:

Record05   0.2 sec   2 Kbyte

Repeats: 5   Trailing silence: 3.0 sec   Total: 17.2 sec

Record has totalled up the five plays of the sample and the five pauses in between, and although it doesn't quite add up as expected (probably due to the round figure given for the size of the sample) in this example, the effect is clear on playback.

A short sample with lots of repeats and not much interval can be effective sound for an alarm. The 'Adjust for alarm' menu option offers a No/Yes dialogue to 'Adjust repeat for use as an alarm'. Press Y and you'll see a change in the Trailing silence figure displayed. In my example the display shows:

Record05   0.2 sec   2 Kbyte

Repeats: 5   Trailing silence: 2.5 sec   Total: 15.0 sec

Specials
The Special menu offers Exit and Set preferences.

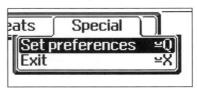

In the latter Playback volume can be Quiet, Medium or Loud (default). Default duration (sec) is 2.0, a bit long for my uses so I've changed down to one second; make your own choice her.

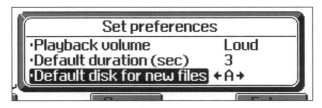

Default disk for new files is Internal but, if you've got additional memory in the form of A or B disks then sound samples should be redirected to them, freeing up your internal disk for application work.

Voice Memo
Having investigated Record pretty thoroughly let's go through the process of recording a voice memo and attaching it to an alarm in Agenda. In this way you can keep a voice memo handy until you need it or you can get Agenda to trigger it at some time in the future as a reminder.

You've no need to worry about attaching the sound sample file initially so you can go into Record, press Tab and Enter and then turn you Psion Series 3 off. You can then keep your Psion Series 3 handy and turn it on when you need to record, turn your Psion Series 3 on and press Space. Speak immediately into the microphone, bearing in mind however long you've given yourself in the Record dialogue and watching the recording progress bar. As often with

Record, it's a good idea to rehearse this technique a few times at home before you use it 'for real'.

Once you've finished the recording, press Tab and Enter again to set up Record for your next memo. In respect of the time available for the memo, I've found that five seconds provides enough time for about a ten word, two phrase, memo.

Attaching this sound sample to an alarm in Agenda or Alarm is simply a matter of using the PsiGuide provided. Alarm pops up a dialogue when you Set alarm and you choose the appropriate sound in the Sound field at the bottom. The same dialogue appears in Agenda.

Sound Stuff

That was Rec...rec...rec...record. I'm sure you'll agree that recording sounds is fun and of some practical use. Now all you need to do is go back to the chapter on Alarm to make your mornings so much more interesting. Wakey wakey!

Chapter 22

Psion Online

Comms[C]

The Psion Series 3's main connection to the outside world is its serial port. By connecting a cable from this port to another computer, a printer or a modem, you are linking your Psion Series 3 to the world beyond. We'll look at how to take advantage of this external connection in a number of ways.

Psion palmtops are tops out in the field and when they come home, you just link them up to your desktop, desk-bound computer. Let's look at moving information from the Psion Series 3 to somewhere else via a cable. The type of cable you'll need differs depending on what device (computer or printer) you are connecting your Psion Series 3 to.

There are three computers which benefit from a Psion product to link them to the Psion Series 3. These are the PC (DOS and Windows), Apple Mac and Acorn RISC OS computers. You can link them with the products PC Link, Mac Link and Alink. For PC Windows users there are two additional bits of software to go with the link cable to choose from: Winlink from Widgit and PsiWin from Psion, which we've already encountered.

You can't easily purchase a serial cable on its own. The Serial Link Cable tends to come with a software product in tow, such as PsiWin. Once you've got the cable, you can then use it for other purposes with other software.

Linking with your desktop computer is useful for making backups of your Psion software and data, to use data you've entered on your Psion Series 3 in software on your desktop, and to share data with colleagues – who may not have a Psion of their own!

Parallel Printing

Because most printers have parallel interfaces and not serial interfaces, it's necessary to have a serial to parallel link if you wish to print directly to a printer. Products such as PsiWin (which prints via your desktop PC), and the infrared data link in Series 3c and Siena, will eventually make the parallel link redundant.

Other Computers

Desktop links connect Psion Series 3 (and Pocket Book II of course) to Acorn 32-bit computers and the Apple Macintosh.

A-Link consists of a cable to connect to the serial port of an Acorn 32-bit computer, a disc containing the PocketFS software which runs under the RISC OS desktop, and a manual. The PocketFS application runs on the Acorn 32-bit computer and provides a view of the files on the Psion or Pocket Book in a RISC OS Filer window. PocketFS incorporates the usual RISC OS 'drag and drop' for file transfer. It looks and feels like any RISC OS filing system, so it makes access to Psion or Pocket Book as easy as to a floppy disc, hard disc or network. It converts files between all the common types, allowing them to be transferred directly between applications on either computer.

Wordprocessors for RISC OS can import and export plain text, and spreadsheets and databases can import and export either CSV or TSV formats or both. In addition, most spreadsheets support WKl, which allows the transfer of the logic of a spreadsheet as well as the data. Some word processors, such as Impression, support RTF, allowing the transfer of some stylistic content such as fonts and highlights.

Application	Input/output for RISC OS/Mac
Write	Plain Text
	RTF (Rich Text Format)
Data (Cards)	CSV (Comma Separated Variable)
	TSV (TAB Separated Variable)
Sheet (Abacus)	CSV (Comma Separated Variable)
	TSV (TAB Separated Variable)
	WK1 (Lotus format)

Table 22.1 A-Link Application Conversion

Using A-Link is straightforward. Connect the cable, run !PocketFS by clicking on the PocketFS icon on the Acorn computer's icon bar. A directory viewer opens. Open the M directory in this directory viewer. Copy the files as specified in the individual installation instructions.

Mac Link for Apple Macintosh consists of a cable with a 9-pin round mini-DIN plug to connect the serial port of the Apple Macintosh computer to Series 3 and Pocket Book. The software provided on 3.5 disk, gives direct access to the disk drives of the Apple Macintosh from Psion Series 3, and supports X and Y modem file transfer protocols. Apple Mac applications have similar input capabilities so Table 22.1 also applies.

Facing Fax

If you can send data down a cable then, by adding a modem, you can send it over the telephone network. The Psion 3Fax is a modem with fax capability. It operates as a send only fax and as a send and receive data modem. It is about half the size of the Series 3, measuring 163mm by 50mm by 23mm. It runs on two AA size batteries.

The fax software can create and send full-sized good-looking faxes. It will format documents complete with cover sheets, company logos and signatures. It will also queue faxes, send them whenever you like, redial engaged numbers and keep a database of telephone numbers.

It's a modem so Psion 3Fax also gives you access to electronic mail (email) and to bulletin boards or on-line computer services, such as Reuters or CompuServe. These services carry vast libraries of information and are especially useful for time-dependent information such as timetables and business news.

Software Only

You no longer have to buy the Psion modem and fax software combination but can buy the 3Fax software bit separately for use with any Group 2 compatible fax modem. Most modems have 2 and 3 compatibility. The software, which is not compatible with the original Series 3, is priced around £50 and comes on SSD disk. It provides the fax software and a cover sheet designer which is a version of Word which can include graphics files in PIC format – essential if you want to get a company logo and/or personal signature at top and bottom.

You can send a fax from within the software or you can 'print' a fax from any application. You just select Fax as the printer model as though it were a real printer. You are prompted for a fax number, recipient name and subject and these details are put into the cover sheet for you.

Up to ten documents can be attached to a fax for sending batches of data. You might use this to send Agenda files to a colleague at work so that they can be placed into your PC desktop diary. The fax software keeps a 50 strong history list, which means you can choose any recently used number and contact details to send a new fax. You can also grab these details from Data. The fax needn't be sent straightaway but can be put off until later, preferably after 1800 hours when it gets cheaper (in the UK) and when you've actually got your fax connected. The Fax Log keeps details of waiting and transmitted faxes with times and data etc.

On-line

If you want to send and receive computer data, you can either connect the Series 3 to the 3-Fax described above, which can transfer data at speeds of up to 2400 bps, or you can connect another modem to any model of the Series 3 using a serial cable (which now comes as part of the PsiWin package) and a multi-modem cable. The latter adapts the serial cable to the popular desktop modems, which can now run at up to 33,600 bps with higher speeds promised for some Internet access.

Both the 3-Fax and the SerialLink cable include a built-in application called Comms which allows you to connect to on-line systems for text display. Most bulletin boards expect an 80 x 25 screen so zoom out to the smallest possible font.

A VT100 Emulator is available separately (from Widgit) on floppy disk for connection to the many other on-line systems which use the more sophisticated VT100 standard. It allows 80 column by 24 line full screen emulation, scalable fonts, Xmodem and Ymodem file transfer and works either with the Serial Link or the Psion 3-Fax modem.

There are several bulletin boards in the UK which stock Psion files. Try Arcade BBS (0181 654 2212), the User Group board (01752 894422), Pacific BBS (01430 431145), Psychotic Mouse (01494 758998) and Digital Databank (01707 323501).

There are shareware offline readers ReadCIX and ReadCIS for use with the CIX and CompuServe systems. You can access these services, download the software once only, install it and then use it to automatically 'collect' information ready for you to browse it offline (i.e. while not connected to the service any longer and therefore not incurring phone charges).

ReadCIS is capable of sending and receiving mail, grabbing messages from your favourite forums and downloading the latest news. It contains a database of CompuServe nodes around the world so you can log on from other climes. A program called WebCIS is available to work in tandem with ReadCIS to access the Internet via CompuServe.

Internet Access

PsiMail Internet is the key piece of software. With this £60 bundle, which runs on Series 3a/3c (512K and above) and requires a standard modem you will be able to manage email and web browsing. Users of the bundled account will be able to download software upgrades free of charge.

As with plain PsiMail you can create, send and receive email messages; including files and documents attached. The suite includes a web browser and a complete set of Internet tools that test if a host is responding, show the route taken by data as it travels across the Internet, obtain information on Internet sites and synchronise the Psion's clock.

PsiMail Internet allows users to access the net through any Internet service provider. For those who do not currently hold an Internet account, the software will run a registration utility that will connect to the Internet via CompuServe Network Services' (CNS) global dial-up network. By using this network, users can get on the net with a local phone call from almost anywhere in the world. Signing up for an Internet account can be done directly from the Psion palmtop through a Set up Wizard.

CNS will support the entire process from receipt of a new request, to establishing a user account and electronic mailbox for that person, to billing the Internet access charges to an individual user. In addition, CNS allows Psion owners to select the alphanumeric mailbox name of their choice, provided it is unique within the Psion Internet domain.

PsiMail Internet Tech Spec

For those thinking of using a provider other than CNS, these are the technical details you may need to quote to your chosen provider. The TCP/IP stack supports: SLIP, PPP, IP, TCP, UDP, ICMP, DNS name resolution, dynamic or static addressing, editable log-in scripts, fixed or mobile connections, smart phone number resolution, telecom charge/calling cards and full hardware handshaking and flow control, baud rates up to 57600 (19200 on Series 3a). The mail software supports: POP3, SMTP transfer protocols, UUE, MIME attachments. The Web browser supports: HTML 2.0, forms, graphics (GIFs), caching, 3 levels of zoom, mail to, saving HTML pages locally, plug in API which allows support for tables and other graphic formats.

Comms

The software that you need for standard communication is something that you already have stored on the 3 Fax or on your Serial Link/PsiWin. To install this software, make sure that your Serial Link or 3 Fax is connected and press System. Press ∪l to display the Install Application window. Move to the Disk prompt and select disk C. Move back to the file name and select Comms.app and press Enter. The icon for Comms will then appear on your System screen.

Other Internet utilities are coming on stream. For instance there's a Web Viewer for reading web pages which you've downloaded from your desktop computer. There are uuencode and uudecode utilities. Uuencoding is a way of wrapping up your files, sending them over the net and then unwrapping them. Check out the web sites in this book's Internet Address Book to find the latest versions of the relevant software. Psion programs aren't big so they download really quickly. See the chapter on Shareware to get an idea of how to install.

Going Mobile

If you want to really go mobile then you can connect your Psion Series 3 to a Nokia mobile telephone, a pager and a satellite tracking system. You'll find that the Psion Series 3 can take full advantage of the telecommunications revolution!

Telenote hooks up to a Nokia 2110 digital mobile telephone connected to the Vodaphone service. You can send short text messages using SMS to phones or PCs. There are some preprepared messages and you can import phone numbers from your existing database. When you receive mail an envelope icon appears on your phone to prompt you to check your Psion. The makers claim that, because of the way the system works, sending a short (160 character) message to any digital phone user costs around five pence. Psion is selling a cable and software bundle to connect up to the Nokia phone at around £50.

Web Sites

If you have access to the Internet from your desktop PC you will want to check out the many worldwide web (WWW). sites relating to Psion matters.

Most browsers support FTP so you can download files (shareware etc) from a web site. The worldwide web is highly graphical and not entirely suitable for browsing on your Psion. However there is much info – such as book texts and databases – which you can download to your PC and thence to your internal disk via PsiWin.

You can gather information and post (leave) information in newsgroups, which are file areas free to everyone to access and arranged around particular subjects. Usenet newsgroups to try are comp.sys.psion.misc or comp.binaries.psion.

Electronic Mail

The Internet is still a text-based means of communications in many ways so your Psion isn't shut out from using it through lack of graphics power. Transferring data along telephone lines has never been that fast in computer terms so text characters are the most efficient way of moving information about. The characters can be ASCII for electronic mail or other forms of text from the keyboard, or hexadecimal numbers for programs and pictures.

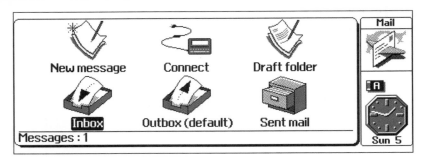

PsiMail is an application which manages electronic mail in a manner similar to that of Microsoft Exchange and it enables your Psion Series 3 to integrate with desktop PC mail systems, both locally in the office and remotely for working at home or in the hotel room.

From	Subject	Date	Size
Ajai	FW: File Manager	05/05/96	1k
	Welcome to PsiMail	05/04/96	1k
Jonathan	RE: FTP server	05/03/96	2k
Darren Wray	Re: Floppies for Psion	05/03/96	2k
Gideon	Internet access with	05/02/96	1k
Microsoft	Welcome!	05/01/96	2k
Jonathan	our letter and press	04/29/96	1k
garyk@soho.ios.	PsiMail	04/27/96	1k

← Inbox →

Messages : 8   Unread Inbox messages : 7

Hints and Tips

If you are using a communications program or file transfer program and you don't press a key and the Psion Series 3 turns off automatically then it will lose contact with whatever it is linked to. When linking up, remember to turn off the auto switchoff option from your System screen.

Chapter 23

Classroom Psion Acorn Pocketbook

The Acorn Pocketbook II is a sister computer to the Psion Series 3. Acorn have naturally configured their Pocket Book II computer somewhat differently for their customers but 90% of the Pocket Book is the same as the Psion model and so Pocket Book owners can happily use this book for their computer. This and the following chapter will address the subtly different aspects and particular uses to which the Pocket Book is put in schools. Psion owners will also find these chapters interesting because they shed light upon practical aspects of using of computer for functions such as data logging.

Looking at the Pocket Book reveals some Acorn green livery and some redesigned icons complete the reworking from an external view. Some renaming has gone on. In line with the terminology used with Acorn's RISC OS desktop computers, the System has been renamed Desktop. Word has been renamed Write, Sheet has been renamed Abacus – and it's got additional graphing facilities – Data is now Cards and Agenda becomes Schedule. Spell – spell checking, dictionary and thesaurus – is also built in. A new application Plotter plots and traces mathematical equations (Cartesian, polar, parametric, etc). Time, World, Calc, Record and OPL Editor remain the same.

One per Child

Acorn Computers has for some time espoused their one computer per child' policy and handheld Pocket Book computers has become a corner stone of this ideal. The idea is that schoolchildren from five to eighteen are likely to have their own palmtop, in the same way as calculators are almost universal now. More common at the moment is for teachers to hand them out at the start of class, collecting them back at the end and then passing them on for another class to use.

The cheaper models of Psion 3a make up the two Pocket Book IIs on offer and Acorn sell them in Class Packs, consisting of 10 Pocket Book IIs , mains adaptor, desktop link and parallel printer link.

There are also School Packs made up of 100 Pocket Book II computers and 10 of each of the peripherals, as well as Site Packs consisting of 1000 Pocket Books, which come with 100 of each peripheral.. All schools that participate in the Tesco Computers for Schools scheme can buy Pocket Books with their vouchers.

Teachers are given the opportunity to try out the Pocket Book free of charge for two months. after two months' trial teachers can either return the Pocket Book II with no obligation, purchase it at the standard price, or, if their school purchases a Class Pack within those two months, keep the Pocket Book free of charge!

The Psion User Group also runs an equivalent Pocket Book User Group (Tel 01752 262627) and free subscriptions are periodically on offer to teachers purchasing Class packs.

Classroom Conduct

The Pocket Book II is good at all the things the Psion Series is, adapted to the academic environment. Pocket Books tend to be integrated into work across the curriculum, which means they are used as 'tools' to help learn any subject rather than being part of a lesson about computers and programming. The idea is that learning to use the Pocket Book will rub off on pupils while they are carrying out their other work.

Some of the uses which the Pocket Book is put to are to collect and record data on field trips, to carry out surveys (eg a class' physical characteristics) and for wordprocessing, including foreign language work. Teachers are using it to record pupil progress and achievement, plan lessons and timetables, draft curriculum materials and take notes in meetings.

Desktop links – to transfer files between Pocket Book II and a desktop computer – allow the Pocket Book II to be used as a mobile data collection device - taking notes and recording information, anywhere and anytime. The data can be downloaded onto a desktop computer for further processing and incorporated into documents for printing, or for communication via networks.

This also allows processing tasks for a project to be divided amongst a number of Pocket Books. In a teaching environment, groups of students can work on a team project, collating the work they have prepared on their Pocket Books on a desktop computer. Moving data in the other direction, teachers can transfer assignments and prepared material from desktop computers to individual Pocket Books.

Pocket Book Products

As mentioned above, the Acorn Pocketbook II is a version of the Psion 3a which is supplied to schools by Xemplar, the joint Acorn/Apple venture. The hardware is pretty much the same as the Psion 3a. In the lists below I've included product codes from the Xemplar catalogue. Bear in mind that these may change in future editions. At the time of writing Pocket Book II offers the choice of two models..

AHB05 Pocket Book II 256K

AHB06 Pocket Book II 512K

Plotter

Plotter is built into the Pocket Book II but is also available separately for Pocket Book upgrading. It is a graph plotting application which fulfils the role of a specialist graphical calculator. It has been designed to meet all curriculum needs in Maths and Science for Key Stages 3 and 4 onwards (11-16) and will also meet most of the requirements for A-level. It is supplied on a ROM SSD with a manual.

AHA44 Plotter

AHA45 Plotter Class Pack (11 Plotters)

Acorn Schedule

Also built into the Pocket Book II but a separate upgrade. Schedule combines a diary, personal organiser and timetabler, and has been designed specifically for the growing number of people in education using the Pocket Book as a personal aid. It is supplied on an SSD ROM card with a manual, and includes the Spell spelling checker so that the two applications still only use one card slot on the Pocket Book.

AHA42 Schedule

AHA11 Schedule Class Pack (11 Schedules)

OPL Editor

Another piece of upgrade software. OPL is a programming language for the Pocket Book. The pack contains all you need to start writing your own programs, and includes a comprehensive manual. Programs are entered using the Program Editor, which is similar to the Write word processor provided with your Pocket Book. To execute a program you have written, you select it from the list of programs displayed on the Desktop screen. Once familiar with the basics you will soon be able to move on to more advanced techniques, including turning your favourite program into an application and installing it onto the Desktop screen.

AHA41 OPL Editor

Pocket Book Peripherals

All the following peripherals work with both the Pocket Book and Pocket Book II.

Desktop Links

Desktop links connect Pocket Book to Acorn 32-bit computers, PC compatibles and Apple Macintosh, providing a quick and easy way of transferring files and data between the two. This extends both the power of Pocket Book and the range of the desktop computer.

AHA30 *A-Link for Acorn 32-bit computers

AHA36 PC Link for IBM PC compatibles

AHA37 M Link for Apple Macintosh

Parallel Link

The Parallel Link connects Pocket Book to a wide range of standard printers. Examples include Canon BJ-10e, Canon BJ-300, IBM Proprinter X24E, Epson RX and Epson LQ. Most dot matrix printers that have an Epson or IBM Proprinter emulation mode can also be used. In addition, Pocket Book also supports a general purpose printer driver that will allow you to print plain text to almost any printer that can accept plain text.

AHA31 Parallel Link

Mains Adaptor

The Mains Adaptor connects Pocket Book to a standard 13 amp mains power supply to provide an alternative power source to the batteries. When used in conjunction with the desktop links, the Mains Adaptor can extend battery life considerably, since the desktop links require significant power to drive the serial port.

AHA35 Mains Adaptor

Solid State Disks (SSDs)

Solid State Disks fit inside Pocket Book and provide additional space for storing information, which can be protected from accidental deletion by moving a write-protect switch.

The RAM SSD has its own lithium battery to retain data and behaves like other random access storage devices such as the standard floppy disc or hard disc: you can read and write files to them and delete some or all of your files, freeing up available space on the SSD.

The RAM SSD is best for storing information that is frequently altered, such as the personal files that you are currently working on. Flash SSDs do not require a back-up battery to retain data, and you can read and write to them, but deleted files still use up space (which can be recovered by reformatting the disc). However, Flash SSDs are more cost-effective than the RAM SSD and are ideal for material you wish to access frequently but seldom change, such as software programs, resources and personal files you wish to archive.

AHA20 RAM Disc 128K

AHA21 Flash Disc 256K

AHA22 Flash Disc 512K

Class Packs

Class Packs make the goal of providing computing power for all students achievable. Each Class Pack includes a set of support peripherals, which are supplied by post to the purchaser on receipt of a completed registration form. One of these items is a desktop link of the purchaser's choice:

A-Link, PC Link or M Link.

Pocket Book II Class Pack

This consists of ten Pocket Book IIs** with an additional Parallel Link,

desktop link and Mains Adaptor.

AHB10 Pocket Book Class Pack

AHB12 Pocket Book II Class Pack

Software

The following is a list of software specifically designed for the Pocketbook and classroom use. Each entry gives the title of the software, the publisher and a brief description with supplier details.

Explorer

Explan

Explorer is an integrated 'Questions and Answers' database for use on project work with class sets of Pocket Books. Lists of questions are prepared on Acorn 32-bit computers and down-loaded onto the Pocket Books. Students use the Pocket Books to record their answers in the field - field trips, museum visits and wildlife walks. The answers are then down-loaded onto the Acorn desktop for assessment, reports and other follow-up work. The software is available as a site licence only, which covers a class pack of 11 Pocket Books.

LogIT Pocket Book Transfer Pack

SCC Research

The LogIT Pocket Book Transfer Pack enables data to be transferred from the LogIT data logger to Pocket Book, where it can be previewed and saved in various formats. The data can then be analysed using the Abacus spreadsheet in table or graph format, and later transferred to a desktop computer.

The Pocket Book Transfer Pack includes site-licensed software on a 3.5" disc and a cable which you attach to your desktop link in order to connect LogIT to Pocket Book. You will also need the LogIT data logger itself. The LogIT Pocket Book Transfer Pack can be ordered from Griffin and George as CRD-140-065G. Griffin and George, Tel 01509 233344

Compute-A-Diet

ComCard

Compute-A-Diet provides a comprehensive nutritional analysis system. It includes values obtained from the Royal Society of Chemistry and MAFF database, which contains 1,188 food entries (with each entry having 36 nutrient values). It has the capability to add records, create recipes, track and analyse diets, and can be used in a number of curriculum areas including Home Economics, IT and PE.

ComCard. Tel 01905 778957

PocketSaC Sense

Data Harvest, Educational Electronics

PocketSac Sense works with Pocket Book to take the Sense and Control realtime interface and data logger into the field. Meter displays fully calibrated values for up to four sensors, allowing the observation of physical change using any of the wide range of analogue sensors available for Sense and Control. Snapshot logging displays calibrated values from all four sensors continuously on the Pocket Book screen, and is particularly useful for environmental data logging. Remote logging allows Sense and Control to be set up for data capture while disconnected from Pocket Book. Captured data can then be retrieved into Pocket Book. Available from Educational Electronics. Tel 01525 373666.

Berlitz Interpreter
Psion

Berlitz Interpreter translates over 28,000 words between five European languages - English, French, Spanish, Italian and German. Any of the five languages can be selected as the source and you can translate between all five, or just two of the languages. Psion. Tel 0171 258 7368.

MiniKeys
NW SEMERC

The MiniKeys application enables a Pocket Book to be used as the keyboard for an Acorn 32-bit computer. This is intended for anyone who has problems with using the standard Acorn

keyboard, including people with limited movement, Repetitive Strain Injury or special needs relating to keyboard entry. NW SEMERC. Tel 0161 627 4469.

Appendix A

....

Software for (nearly) Free

Where commercial companies fear to tread, shareware and freeware fills the void. Check out the cheap (but not nasty) end of the market.

A dedicated band of programmers is constantly coming up with new utilities, games and leading edge software for the Psion range and in this chapter I'll explain how Public Domain and shareware software works and bring you news of some of the best of this type of software available for your Psion Series 3.

Everyone reacts positively when they see FREE displayed in a shop window or in a magazine advert. But there's always a sneaking suspicion that nothing in life is free! This applies to the world of public domain and shareware on the Psion Series 3.

Public domain (PD) programs are made freely available to all Psion Series 3 owners by their authors. They are passed on through personal contact and through PD libraries. Shareware programs are made available by their authors for free trial but the programs must be paid for if used for any longer than a specified period.

So many programs are swimming about in the PD and shareware software ocean, just waiting to be fished out. But there are two costs: firstly you have to pay a PD library to duplicate the programs onto a disc and to send it out properly packaged and with the correct postage; secondly you have to spend time searching the columns of magazines to find the program you want. The actual program is free but the extras are not.

Nevertheless PD and shareware is very good value for all Psion Series 3 owners and is an excellent way to start your interest in computing. You will be receiving programs proudly submitted to the PD libraries by programmers who have created an application or a utility which they feel is good enough for public exposure.

OPL

One of the sources of Psion's long-lasting success and the reason that so many programs are available for their palmtops is their inclusion of OPL, the BASIC like programming language, in the Series 3 computer. Having OPL on-board has resulted in thousands of applications being written for Psion handhelds. OPL is simple to use if you have used BASIC on a desktop computer or can spare a few hours to learn the principles. On the other hand Psion would claim that OPL also offers powerful features to challenge the most experienced programmer.

There are two parts to OPL, the editor where you create the program in the form of a list of commands and the runtime version of the code, which results from your commands, and presents itself to the user of the program. In OPL a programmer can create an application that looks, feels, and most importantly, works like the built in applications.

Sources

The PD librarian plays an important role in sieving the material available and it is common for a library to specialise in a particular type of PD, music files for instance, and a library will have a demonstration disc to give a flavour of what it offers.

Another excellent source of software are the special forums on on-line systems like CompuServe and from sites on the Internet which specialise in Psion Series 3 coverage. The places to look on CompuServe are the two palmtop forums. There are PDA (Personal Digital Assistant) sites on the Internet, many with Psion departments.

Use the Find icon in your CompuServe browser to locate interesting forums through keywords such as 'palmtop' or use a search engine on the Internet to get the latest sites applicable to your interests.

There are two fundamental types of free software available for the Psion Series 3. These are the definitions so you know what you are dealing with when ordering and it is important, especially when purchasing shareware, to follow the etiquette.

Public Domain/Freeware

This software carries the copyright of the author. The author has given his/her permission for you to freely copy the software and pass it on to other users as long as:

- No files that it contains are deleted or changed.

- No files are added.

- Further wishes of the author may be contained in a text file and these should be adhered too. If you wish to use or change any part of a public domain program it best to write to the author and ask for permission. If no address is contained within the program, make sure that you give the original author credit.

Shareware

The standard rules of shareware are:

- You may freely distribute copies of the software to other users.

- You have a 30 day trial period to evaluate the software.

- If, after this time limit, you are still using the software or intend to use it in the future then you must register with the author and pay any registration fee due. You are breaking the law if you fail to do so.

- If you do not intend using the software then you must delete it from your floppy/hard disc.

So now you know where you stand. You may well find more conditions within the program itself or in a help/text file. This is increasingly the case as shareware is more and more used as a legitimate method of software distribution. I haven't heard of any shareware millionaires yet but you never know, the time may come.

Getting Software

There are a number of easy ways of getting hold of public domain and shareware software:

- By copying colleagues' discs.

- By sending off to a PD/shareware distributor or library.

- From magazine discs.

- From a bulletin board via the telephone.

Copying from friends and colleagues is the quickest and cheapest way of obtaining material. Unlike normal commercial software, for which passing between parties is illegal, you are positively encouraged to copy them. Shareware authors desire the widest possible distribution, as this increases the number of people who may possibly register.

Choosing PD is a matter of scouring the magazine adverts or sending off to the PD libraries for their sampler or library disc, possibly for a nominal fee. This disc may contain some actual PD or it may be packed with lists of PD programs. The more ambitious catalogue discs have quite sophisticated presentations and the most useful have full descriptions of the programs. Your aim, as far as possible, is to find out what you are buying. Each disc in the catalogue has an identification number which you use when ordering so note down the numbers of any discs that interest you.

Watch out for duplication of material because some libraries compile their own collections, of utilities, pictures etc, which are taken from existing discs in the catalogue. If you are dealing with more than one library then this becomes more difficult to check. Most libraries don't do a pick and mix service so you have to buy the disc with 20 printer programs on it because it's got the one you want even though you will immediately delete the other 19 because you've already got them.

When initially distributed, the idea is that shareware is on approval, effectively a free trial. Each program will contain information about registration and a disc based text file providing enough documentation to allow you to use it effectively. Registration means that you pay a more realistic price for the software, by sending payment to the author. In return, you will receive the benefits of a normal, commercially available package, such as updates, printed manuals, extra facilities and so on. If you don't like the software and therefore don't use it you don't have to part with any cash. A true case of the software author putting his mouth where is money is.

Because you, the customer, are dealing directly with the author, the registration fee is much lower than the cost of similar commercial packages. Naturally, registration is a matter of trust, and no-one is going to know if you don't register. However, if you are serious about a particular shareware program, you are likely to want the full documentation and extras that are available, so there is a natural incentive to register. Indeed the products are often so good that you want to register to receive future updates.

Payment is not the problem. Most of the authors will accept Access and Visa card payments, or have European agents. International Money Orders and Eurocheques are readily available for a small charge at your local bank.

Distribution

Shareware distributors come in all shapes and sizes, from hobbyists doing it for fun, to highly professional firms with large and detailed catalogues. Naturally, a professional firm employing staff and printing catalogues will have more overheads, so you might expect to pay a little more per disc for the material. Costs range from about £1.50 to £10 per disc, although virtually all the distributors at the higher price bracket reduce the unit price if you order several discs at once. In practice, the cost of blank media plus duplication is usually the smaller part of the distributors' overheads, the larger part being staff to fulfil orders and answer telephone calls, and advertising and printing.

There is, incidentally, no law preventing anyone actually making a profit from shareware distribution, but natural competition has brought the charges to a very fair level. Some distributors have a club system, whereby as a member, you obtain better prices.

Many authors have actually specified a maximum charge (usually $10) to be made for the distribution of their disc, and shareware distributors generally have charges which are below these levels. Some authors even go as far as to specify that no charge whatsoever may be made – you will normally only find these programs on bulletin boards, or bundled on discs with other programs, as even blank floppies cost money!

Most shareware distributors have no involvement with the author registration process, and once you have purchased discs from them, that is the end of it – if you want to obtain updates, you have to contact the author direct.

Disks and Downloads

Psion Series 3 programs are often distributed on PC disks because it's the cheapest way so you'll need to learn the skills of copying programs from your PC disk drive to your Psion Series 3. See the chapters on PsiWin and the appendix on third-party software.

You can download directly from a bulletin board or service such as CompuServe if you are a member. CompuServe is changing the underlying interface of their system as we go to press and this may effect availability to Psion Series 3 users so do check Psion Series 3 compatibility with CompuServe, or any other on-line service, before joining. You'll still be able to download to a PC and then transfer of course. CiX is another popular spot for Psion users. The chapter on Comms will fill you in on more detail on how about going on-line with your Psion 3a.

When you download a file or get it on PC floppy disk you'll probably find that the files you need to send to your Psion are 'packaged' inside a zip file. There is an unzip utility for the Psion, written by Jochen Siegenthaler, but you may find it more convenient to do your unzipping on the PC before sending the files to your Psion, using either PKunzip from DOS or Winzip from Windows.

PsiGuide begins... Unzipping a file

If you download a file from a bulletin board or a FTP site, or if you purchase a Psion program on a PC format disk, then you may receive the Psion files as a collection wrapped up in a single zip file. A compression program called PKzip has been used to wrap up all the files together and to compress them at the same time.

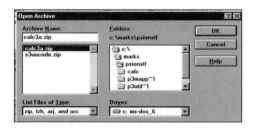

Use a utility such as PKunzip or Winzip to open the zip file (which will have a .zip suffix) and to extract the individual files onto your hard disk. You must then copy these files to your Psion Series 3 via a link cable and program. These are covered in the chapters on PsiWin and Making Links.

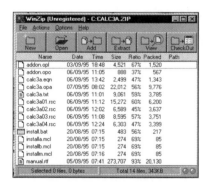

Amongst the files in the zip file you will find a Readme text file which you can load into a wordprocessor (Windows Notepad or Write). This will give instructions on which files you need to copy to the Psion Series 3 and how to install the files as an application which will appear on your System screen. If you are in doubt check the chapter in this book on System Setup.

PsiGuide ends

PD Software is often distributed in a compressed format so you may have to run a decompressor utility before you can use it, either on a PC before sending the program to your Psion Series 3 or on your Psion Series 3 itself. Although it's cheap, it's still annoying if a disc corrupts during this process, so take a copy beforehand. If you decompress on the PC first then you can take the programs that you really need and send them to your Psion Series 3. There is even a Shareware CD-ROM with over 400 Psion programs on it. CD-ROM is a very neat way of keeping lots of files to hand but the programs will get out of date if the CD-ROM is not regularly updated and republished.

PD provides lots of ways to make your Psion Series 3 that bit different through startup screens, clocks, alternative calculators etc. You get the idea. There is also plenty of scope for entertainment through board games, arcade shoot'em ups and the rest.

More useful are utilities for compressing files to save space on your disks, backing up files, recovering accidental deletions and so on. Some PD is very specialised, eg a houseplant finder which can choose a suitable houseplant for your lighting and temperature conditions. This kind of PD can prove a fantastic find if it suits your interests, but is otherwise meaningless.

There follows a short list of typical PD programs you might wish to investigate. There's also some contact information for places to find PD and Shareware for your Psion Series 3.

Reader

by Barry Childress

Shareware $20 registration

Internet: 73510.1420@compuserve.com

Text versions of classic novels etc are available through project Gutenberg on the Internet or CompuServe. Reader can be used to view these books on screen, to add bookmarks, compress the files, search the text and read vertically on screen.

Mapper-3a
by Steve Litchfield

Shareware £14 registration

Map of the UK with hundreds of overlays which provide townplans, county boundaries, airfields, National Trust properties, hotel chains and so on.

Mac System

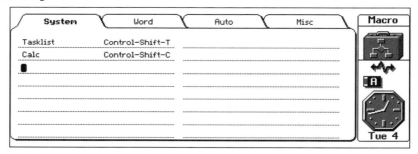

Create your own hot-keys and record tasks for push button replaying.

Memovoc2
Voice memo manager for recording and playing back voice memos.

Charm

An easy way to access the many special, non-keyboard, characters which are in the fonts inside your Psion Series 3.

Month View

Sun	Mon	Tue	Wed	Thu	Fri Shalini	Sat
			1	2	3	4
5	6	7	8	9	10	11
12	13	14	15 Vikki	16	17	18
19	20	21	22 Jaya	23	24	25 **May 21 1996**
26	27	28	29	30	31	

The View that Psion forgot to put into the Psion Series 3a version of Agenda, although Series 3c and Siena owners have already got what they need courtesy of a new version.

JBSort

```
                  Select Search Fields
   Field            ← Co: →
  ·Field            Name:
  ·Field            ☎ Tel:
  ·Destination Name  Nwt.dbf
  ·          Disk   Internal
  ·Direction        Forward
  ·Stay/Leave       Leave
```

A straightforward sort program for Data files.

Freeware/Shareware Libraries

There are a number of independent libraries which cater for the Psion user. Cross check also with the list of user groups in the appendix on Psion clubs. These clubs often run their own shareware lists.

3-Lib

According to 3-Lib, well over one thousand items for the Siena, Series 3 and 3a are available as public domain software or shareware. The programs available range from file management utilities to a complex database manager to a full GB mapping product to a home-banking system to a wide variety of games.

Steve maintains a Web site which contains a multitude of reviews of the available programs so you can read up on them to decide which ones you want.

Orders can be shipped out on floppy disk (for those of you with serial links and desktop computers) or ready-to-run on SSD by special arrangement.

For a free information pack, just send a loose 1st class stamp plus an A4 or A5 stamped, self-addressed envelope. If you're outside the UK, send equivalent international reply coupons etc. You can also visit the 3Lib web site.

Contact Steve Litchfield at 3-Lib, 22 Grays Crescent, Woodley, Berks, RG5 3EN, Great Britain.Tel: +44 (0)1734 265081.

Appendix B

Clubs and Contacts

Owning a Psion Series 3 is a statement of intent: to get to grips with this new technology that can govern, but also liberate. And you are not alone. Psion Series 3 owners tend to club together to share information and experience. The Psion Series 3 has so much potential that applications and approaches for its use are appearing daily. Sharing information is a way of not reinventing the wheel and of helping beginners get up to speed faster than through struggling in isolation.

You'll find that there are hundreds, nay thousands, of enthusiasts with Psion Series 3 experience who are willing to share their expertise and admit to where they went wrong in order to make your life a bit easier.

There are two types of club: local and by mail. Local groups tend to meet every month and to have a theme for each get-together. They put on demonstrations and invite companies to come and show their new creations. Secondhand auctions at Christmas and training sessions are also among the common activities of a local computer club. Check the magazines and the diary of events in your local press to find your nearest club. You'll find that all kinds of computer are owned by members of the local club and you may therefore join – or begin – a special user group within the club structure, getting the best of both worlds.

Club Contacts

By mail groups tend to be based upon a common interest in Psion Series 3. Some are involved in producing newsletters or magazines, some provide a PD/Shareware service too. You may find that the club runs on a swap basis or that there's a modest subscription.

Palmtop

Palmtop, 25 Avocet Way, Bicester, Oxon, OX6 0YN, England.

Tel: +44 (0)1869 249287

Fax: +44 (0)1869 249287

Email: sclack@cix.compulink.co.uk

100602.3723@compuserve.com

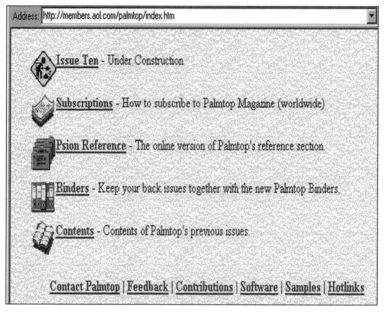

Palmtop is a bi-monthly (six per year) magazine with 60+ pages (A5) of news, reviews and helpful tutorials and hints and tips. Editor, Steve Clack. A single issue costs £4 Uk and £5 elsewhere. Annual subscription costs £24 UK, £27 Europe and £33 elsewhere. Payment in UK funds, credit cards accepted.

Psion User Group

Psion User Group, Sliddery House, 31 Toor View Avenue, Peverell, Plymouth, Devon, PL3 4QN.

Tel: 01752 262627

Hotline : 01752 781818

Fax: 01752 769621

BBS: 01752 894422

When you join the Psion User Group you get a membership card with helpline number for unlimited technical support. The newsletters are 12-14 pages and there are single page A4 newsheets in the months between the quarterly frequency.

Help line, bulletin board and Internet site. If you don't have a modem the club will download programs onto your SSD at a cost of £10.00 for three programs or £8.00 onto a floppy disc. Training videos £29.50 each.

Seminars have been held in edinburgh, Birmingham and London and the club has regional representatives. £36 per annum approximately. Also runs the Acorn Pocket Book equivalent.

Datalink Bulletin Board
BBS: 01202 660838

Internet: vui@cix.compulink.co.uk

Club Série 3
Club Série 3, 6 rue de Fecamp, 75012, Paris, France.

Tel: +33 140049219

Fax: +33 143072596

BBS: +33 143331547

E-mail: debeau@ellis.fdn.org

Club with magazine and bulletin board. Annual subscription 200 French francs.

South Pacific
Australian South Pacific Psion Series 3 User Group, c/o Roslyn Copas, 113/382, Ruthven St, Toowoomba, QLD 4350, Australia.

Tel: +61 418 717281

Fax: +61 76 321081

An independent user group with its own User News newsletter four times per year. User phone support is available and the club provides freeware and shareware for just A$1 per disk. Annual subscription for Australia is A$20, for elsewhere A$23. The group committee comprises Duncan Schultz, Roslyn Copas and Luke Hughes.

Appendix C

Internet Address Book

Use your desktop PC to access the Internet where there are many sites covering the use of your Psion Series 3, together with news, hints and tips and gossip about your favourite palmtop. Download information and then use PsiWin to move programs and data across to your Psion Series 3. Please remember that Internet addresses often change. If you have a problem with any of the addresses below then use a search engine such as Yahoo! to search for 'Psion' or 'palmtop'. Most sites contain a 'links' section to take you to other interesting sites. So once you've found a good Psion site, use its links to find other similar places to visit on the Net.

Address Book

Internet sites for Psion owners

http://ourworld.compuserve.com/homepages/slitchfield/

http://www.bris.ac.uk/%7Elwmdcg/Psion/

http://www.bris.ac.uk/%7Elwmdcg/Psion/FAQ

http://www.geocities.com/SiliconValley/8130/

http://www.geocities.com/SiliconValley/8130/prgers.htm

http://www.primate.wisc.edu/people/dubois/psion/oplman/index.html

http://www.cityscape.co.uk/users/cdwf/psion/psionics

http://intertrader.com/computers/clove/

http://www.widget.co.uk/

http://intertrader.com/computers/clove/

http://www.nwt.com

http://www.psion.com

http://www.psioninc.com/

http://emporium.turnpike.net/P/psion-gmbh/

http://www.acorn.co.uk/acorn/

http://www.compulink.co.uk/~jbsoft

http://ourworld.compuserve.com/homepages/chocolate_island_software/

http://ourworld.compuserve.com/homepages/pelican/

http://ourworld.compuserve.com/homepages/psipple/

http://ourworld.compuserve.com/homepages/groucho/

http://ourworld.compuserve.com/homepages/andyc

http://ourworld.compuserve.com/homepages/pelican/

http://ourworld.compuserve.com/homepages/mobile_pages

http://ourworld.compuserve.com/homepages/g0hzk

http://ourworld.compuserve.com/homepages/alanrichey/

http://www.compulink.co.uk/~djoyce

http://www.innomate.de/lansys/psioman/

http://members.aol.com/palmtop

http://www.u-net.com/~vikingc/psion3a.htm

http://www.worldonline.nl/~rschmidt/

http://ourworld.compuserve.com/homepages/matt_thomas/

http://www.symantec.com/compinfo/news/products/actpispr.html

http://ourworld.compuserve.com/homepages/swebb

http://dialspace.dial.pipex.com/john.whiting/

http://www.compulink.co.uk/~windmill/

International

http://www.hkstar.com/micro/	China
http://alex_union-fin.fr/usr/dcabuzel/psion/clubpsion.html	France
http://www.datanet.hu/internetto/ads/psion/	Hungary
http://www.wave.cube.net/	Germany
http://www.nicolas.com	UK User Group
http://www.hkstar.com/lmicro	Digital Vision has info, shareware and screenshots in English and Chinese.
http://www.cent.saitama-u.ac.jp/lmasaaki/psion/	Masaaki Fujiyoshi, a student at Saitama Uni runs this japanese Psion page
http://cipserv.ikm.uni-mannheim.de/mtr/psion.html	Klein und Clever ist eine seite zum Psion
http://www.wave.cube.net/puc.html	Der Psion User Club
http://alex.union-fin.fr/usr/dcabuzel/psion/psion.html	For French readers
http://wwwbris.ac.uk/%7elwmdcg/psion/	Hot Psion links

Usenet Newsgroups

comp.sys.psion.announce

comp.sys.psion.apps

comp.sys.psion.marketplace

comp.sys.psion.misc

comp.sys.psion.programmer

comp.sys.psion.reviews

comp.binaries.psion

FTP Sites

ftp://src.doc.ic.ac.uk/packages/psion/icdoc/

ftp://ftp.frontiernet.net/pub/psion

To get the Frequently Asked Questions (FAQ) document, send an email to mail-server@rtfm.mit.edu with the message containing the words help and index. Instructons will be mailed to you.

Appendix D

Highly Tech

 This appendix is highly technical and is provided to give some idea of how your Psion Series 3 works beneath the bonnet, so to speak. The descriptions owe much to Psion's own documentation about their software and is reproduced by me without any comment. Although this appendix contrasts with the style of the rest of the book, I think you may find it interesting, even if you don't understand it all!

SIBO and EPOC

Psion give their family of handheld computers the name SIBO. This family includes the Series 3, Series 3a, Series 3c, HC and Workabout.

Psion pride themselves on packing a lot into small amounts of memory and the job of the SIBO operating system architecture is to make it possible to write high quality applications which demand memory in tens of kilobytes rather than in megabytes.

Although development on the SIBO platform started in 1987, it has many modern features such as asynchronous services and pre-emptive multi-tasking.

All SIBO machines run the same operating system and use the same built-in library code. This allows developers to write programs that will work, without recompilation, on the entire SIBO range.

SIBO Architecture

A SIBO machine is a battery-powered portable computer that is based on the SIBO architecture. This architecture is designed to minimise the size, weight and power consumption of the computer. The key components of the architecture are:

- a sophisticated power management system that selectively powers subsystems under software control.

- Solid State Disks (SSDs) that provide fast low-power silicon-based mass storage with no moving parts.

- a synchronous serial interface for peripherals running at high speed (Mega bit rates).

- an 8086-family processor.

- hardware protection of the system from aberrant processes (address trapping of out-of-range writes and a watch-dog timer on interrupts being disabled).

- real-time clock.

- ROM-resident system software.

- graphical, low-power LCD display.

- digital sound recording, processing and replay system (used in some models).

The hardware architecture is primarily implemented in custom ICs called ASICs. Construction uses surface-mounted static CMOS ICs throughout.

Software Components

The following components are built into the ROM of a SIBO machine:

- EPOC – a pre-emptive multi-tasking operating system.

- PLIB – a runtime library similar to the ANSI C standard libraries, but optimised for SIBO.

- device drivers that provide access to a wide range of devices from RS-232 serial ports to timers.

- the window server – a server process that provides fast, low-level graphics, fonts and windowing services.

- Object Libraries – a set of classes that can be used with Psion's C-based OOP (Object-Oriented Programming) system (not included in HC computers).

These components provide an extremely rich programming environment for applications and the results are available to the Psion Series 3 user.

EPOC-making

EPOC is the pre-emptive, multi-tasking operating system used on all SIBO hand-helds, capable of handling 24 simultaneous processes.

One immediate consequence of multi-tasking is that users are never barred from switching to another task, even if the current application is busy. You never see the equivalent of the Mac wristwatch or the Windows hourglass. EPOC actually stops the processor clock when the system is idle, thus saving power.

Asynchronous Services

Without asynchronous services, it is difficult to write an application that responds to more than one event source. For example, the Agenda application on the Series 3a does not know whether its next event will be a key press or the expiry of an alarm.

The provision of asynchronous events makes it easier to write programs that always respond to user input. EPOC supports asynchronous requests for such things as inter-process messaging and timers.

Managing Memory

The SIBO architecture is built around the 80x86 processor family. The 8086 uses 64K segments that can either contain code or data. EPOC programs are written using the small memory model where there is one data segment and one code segment. Because the programs themselves do not access the segment registers, EPOC is able to provide memory management in software by moving, re-sizing, allocating and freeing segments.

A process can build data structures in excess of 64K by using external memory segments and programs of greater than 64K can be built using dynamic link libraries (DYLs).

The SIBO hardware provides a write-protection safety catch on memory segments not owned by the process. Any process writing outside its own data segment is terminated by the operating system.

EPOC will give more memory to an application and will also reduce it if possible if that allocated memory is subsequently freed, which leads to extremely efficient use of the system RAM.

The PLIB library

PLIB is a runtime library, similar to the ANSI C standard libraries. All the library functions are fully re-entrant so that they can be accessed (apparently) simultaneously by many processes. All programs have access to this library and therefore do not need to contain any library code themselves. Industrial-strength error handling is provided by all the functions in the library.

Device Drivers

EPOC provides a layered device driver system. Device drivers can be loaded and unloaded without the need to reboot. Each driver can be connected to another so that a stack of drivers can be constructed.

Many I/O devices are built into the ROM - for example, a comprehensive RS232 device and a parallel port device.

File System

File services are implemented by a file server. Each process is automatically made a client of the file server when loaded. The local file store itself is based on a MSDOS-compatible directory hierarchy.

An installable file system is used to remote file servers which have been implemented for PC and Apple Mac.

Client-server

EPOC has very efficient inter-process communication services that provide good support for multi-process applications with client-server architectures. Two servers are built into the ROM (the window server and the file server).

Object-oriented

EPOC contains run-time support for object oriented programming. A subset of that support can also be used to implement code-sharing dynamic link libraries.

Window server

The window server is a system server process that runs under EPOC to provide client application processes with shared access to the screen and keyboard. Using a server process is a common way of managing access to shared, serially-reusable resources.

The window server provides the necessary mechanisms for a graphical user interface but not the user interface itself. Any number of different interface styles can be built using the window server. The user interface used by Psion's programs is defined by built-in object-oriented class libraries.

Events

The window server sends its clients events which drive the user interface. Event types include key press events (which are sent to the foreground task), redraw events, foreground and background events.

Windows

The window server supports a hierarchical window system. Once created, windows may be moved, resized, made visible or invisible or scrolled in any direction. Windows may overlap and drawing is clipped to the visible area of a window.

When areas of a window are exposed by the movement, change in size, or the removal of other windows, appropriate redraw events are sent to notify the application of invalidated areas. The application's redrawing of an invalid area is automatically clipped to those parts that need to be redrawn. Windows may be assigned a back-up bitmap to avoid the application having to process redraw events itself.

Graphics

Graphics operations include line and box drawing, filled rectangles, text drawing with a variety of bitmap fonts and textual attributes, and general bitmap operations. All operations are written in speed-tuned assembler. Drawing is normally directed at a window but can also be directed to a bitmap.

The built-in fonts and bitmaps can be extended by external fonts and bitmaps. External bitmaps are used, for example, to implement icons.

RAM Usage

EPOC was designed to allow SIBO programs to use as little RAM as possible. This is achieved by:

- code sharing – if more than one copy of a program is run the code segment for the progam is not loaded again. Instead the processes share the same code segment.

- library code – using ROM-based library functions means programs only have to contain application-specific code.

- execute-in-ROM – programs built into the ROM do not have to be loaded into RAM to be run (unlike many other operating systems).

- client-server – the window and file server provide graphics and I/O services to all other processes, so this code does not have to be included in every program.

Appendix E

Hardware and Software Products

Psion palm-tops get top-notch support from third party manufacturers and software publishers. In other words, there are plenty of new toys to buy for your continued Psion Series 3 pleasure. Here are just some of the products which you might wish to put on your wish list or birthday/Christmas present hint list! The lists have been compiled by information current at the time so do contact the suppliers for up to date information.

Hardware

This is the stuff which you can touch and feel. The Psion itself comes in different configurations and value for money in the memory stakes is certainly found at the top end of the range. You might wish to trade in and up. Perhaps another family member can take your old Psion off your hands or are you reading this book because you're on the lookout for a secondhand Psion?

Add-ons

There's not much room, but it wouldn't be a computer if you couldn't add bits on! The Psion Series 3 proves itself remarkable once again by having considerable potential for expansion. You can add both internal memory expansion and external peripherals such as fax modem and floppy disk drive. There's even a big keyboard so your Psion Series 3 becomes a docking station! Watch out that the add-on is designed for your particular model of Psion. There are sometimes different versions for Series 3, 3a and 3c and the Siena is a different design and often needs different components.

Expansion

You've already got a lot to be getting on with this new computer. In the future however you may wish to enhance its performance to help you achieve something specific.Read on to find out about about the possible upgrades, add-ons and peripherals.

Hardware is expensive and you've already got a lot of high technology under your belt with the Psion Series 3 itself so you might not be intending to update or upgrade, although it rather depends on which computer you do have. All of us however are in the market for the more interesting add-ons in life, even if it's just window shopping part of the time.

This pocket guide to hardware extensions to your computing repertoire skims the surface of what is available. Technology changes constantly so check your magazines and local dealers to see what's new.

The computer software which Psion provide with the Psion Series 3 has a sophisticated look about it, with icons and menus etc. But this user-interface is sitting on top of the operating system which is a set of programs which glue together parts of the computer system such as the keyboard and serial port.

When the Psion Series 3 OS can handle an add-on then you can go out and buy one, and not before.

A common term when talking about upgrading is add-*on* but this more properly describes boxed units which plug onto external connectors

Extra memory for instance is usually an add-*in*.

Peripherals

There are two categories of peripheral. The first includes external keyboards and disk drives, which are specific to the Psion Series 3. You can't buy off the shelf PC type units, at least not without the appropriate adaptors.The second category encompasses more generalised add-ons, usually available for all computers, not just the Psion Series 3, such as printers and modems.

Portable printers

There's no doubt how portable the Psion Series 3 is but what about the add-ons? If you are on the road and you need a printout, this is a potential problem. Weight matters because you'll need to carry it with you and you'll need power , preferably batter but with the ability to recharge. On the other hand the quality of the printout has got to be up to scratch. Otherwise you wouldn't be bothering. Are quality and portability mutually incompatible?

HP DeskJet 340

A 600 x 300 dpi inkjet, the 340 is more for the car or hotel room than the briefcase. It weighs 1.94kg, has a parallel port and 64K memory on board. It measures 31cm x 14.7cm x 6.5cm. The £18 black and white cartridge lasts about 750 pages and the colour (£35) around 400 pages. This is the kind of printer you might buy if you want to use it both with your desktop PC and your Psion Series 3. It's fast and the printout quality is great.

Citizen PN60

Claimed to be the world's smallest and lightest and to have 'laser quality'. It's 500g, measures 25.4 cm x 5.05 cm x4.7 cam and it can print on plain paper, labels and OHP slides. This is a thermal printer with 360 dpi resolution, which is what is meant by 'laser' I suppose. A £5.99 black ribbon lasts 3500 character or around 30 A4 pages. There's a colour kit and each four colour ribbon costs £8.99. There's 64K memory on board and the emulations are Epson LQ, NEC and IBM ProPrinter.

The PN60 is powered from a slim power adapter or an (optional) rechargeable NiCAd battery, which lasts about 50 pages, longer than the ribbon!

The PN60 interface is parallel but Citizen can supply a connectivity kit to link their PN60 to the Psion Series 3 and Acorn Pocketbook. Citizen Europe Tel 01753 584111.

The PN60 is a good match for the Psion Series 3 although the printout quality is ordinary.

Pentax PocketJet

Thermal technology once again but printing only on fax style paper at £6 per 100 sheets. The resolution is 300 dpi and there's no colour option. The unit has a NiCad battery built in and weights 497g. It measures 3 cm x 25.5 cm x 5.5 cm. The power supply is as big as the printer but the battery provides for 30 pages and you can carry a second battery with you. Emulation is HP Laserjet IIP, for which there's a Psion driver. The printer's parallel port autodetects the optional serial cable. Highly suitable except for the large power supply.

Keyboard

You can connect a PC keyboard to your Psion Series 3 via the 3Link cable. The adapter costs £55 and a compact keyboard is available for a further £55. The adapter is powered by a battery or Psion Series 3 main power supply.

Dr Keith R Baker, 61 Alderhill Drive,Totton,Southampton,Hants,SO40 8JB.
Email: krb"ecs.soton.ac.uk. Tel:+44 (0)1703 864310.

Accessories

3Link (PC serial link)		Psion
Winlink		Widget
3Link (Mac serial link)		Psion
Parallel (print) link		Psion
Mains adaptor		Psion
Leather case		Psion
Carry case		Psion
3Fax (fax modem)		Psion
Mains Adaptor		Psion
PSIWIN (RS232) for PC		Psion
Serial Link (RS232) Apple Mac Version		Widget
Conversion kit for PC Serial Link to Apple Mac Version		Widget
Desk Holder for 5 SSDs ('Toast Rack')		Widget
3 FAX — complete kit incl. software, cable and modem		Psion
Telephone adaptors — all EC Countries + US		Widget
Telephone adaptors — Australia, NZ, US, Pacific Islands		Widget
Parallel Link		Widget
Multi/modem cable (connects Serial Link or MC to a modem)		Widget
Dual 9/25 way connector for 3-link		Widget
Black Anodised Aluminium Desk Stand		Widget
3-Bar kit for the Series 3/3a (3 Bar and 3 Wand)		Widget
SSD drive system		Psion
Solid State Disks (SSDs)		Psion
Flash	128K	
	256K	
	512K	
	1Mb	
	2Mb	
	4Mb	
RAM	128K	
	512K	
	1Mb	

Batteries

Backup
1620 3v Lithium
Main
2 x 1.5v

Software

You are not restricted to using only the programs which come with your Psion 3a. There are many useful and entertaining programs which you can purchase. Most of these work on the full range of Psion Series 3 computers although some require 512K RAM to function. Some recent programs – such as Soundmaster – are only compatible with the Psion 3a.

Programs from a PC

Another way of loading a program into your Psion Series 3 is to use your PsiWin and/or PC link to upload (load from outside the Psion Series 3) a program from another computer. In this way you can buy the program on a PC format floppy disk or even on a CD-ROM and then load it via the PC.See the chapter on PsiWin and Comms for more details.

Applications

Psion Series 3 SSD

Business

Program	Supplier
Personal Accounts and Expenses	Psion
Money	Psion
Financial Calculator	Psion
3 Base	Psion
Data deLuxe	Psion
Phrasebook	Berlitz
Interpreter	Berlitz
Spellchecker & Thesaurus	Psion
Spreadsheet	Psion
Finance Pack	Widget
Agenda Link	Widget
Toolkit	Purple
Hermit by 3X communications	(tel 01756 700025)
Remote access to host AS/400 computer.	
Notepad Deluxe	Purple
Series 3 Tools (Filemanager and Convert)*	Widget
Paint and Compose*	Widget
Kallcost and Phoneday (on SSD)*	Widgit
Datadeluxe v2.5*	Widgit
Dataview*	Widget
Timebase*	Widget
Flochart*	Widgit
Orgchart*	Widget
Sightmaster 3	Widget

Program	Supplier
Tideclock 3	Widget
Spreadsheet (for Series 3 Classic only)	Widget
Autoroute Express (US version available)	Psion

Entertainment

Pipemania	Psion
Games 1, 2, 3a	Psion
Chess	Psion
Hugh Johnson's Wine Guide	Psion
Backgammon/Chinese Chess	Purple
Paint and Compose	Widget
Comcard Compute-a-diet	Widgit

PC CD-ROM

Shareware CD-ROM (Volume 1)	Widget
Shareware CD-ROM (Volume 2)	Widget

PC floppy

WINlink v2.0	Widget
Agenda Link v2	Widget
Agenda Link 20 user licence	Widget
Soundmaster.	Psion
OPL Development Environment	Psion
VT100 Emulator V2.8* (3a only)	Widget
Timebase	Widget
Kallcost and Phoneday	Widget
Commander 3a	Widget
ACT! (3a only)	Psion
Expotel Hotel Guide	Widget
Finance Pack 3a (3a only)	Widget
Finance Pack 3 (Series 3 Classic version)	Widget
Psion Money (3a only)	Psion
Financial Calculator (was Professional Finance)*	Widget
Widget Games Pack 3a (3a only)	Widget
Psion Games Pack 3a (3a only)	Psion
PipeMania*	Widget
Chess	Psion
Widget Games Pack 3	Widget
Psion Games Pack 2	Psion
Psion Games Pack 1	Psion
Lost Treasures of Infocom (on floppy disk)	Psion

UK Contacts

If you are trying to keep up to date with Psion-related products then a magazine such as Palmtop can help you with news and product reviews. The products listed here will soon be joined by new applications and updates. To help you get the information you need, here are the main points of contact for Psion product. Many computer retailers carry Psion products but these contacts represent the main specialists.

Psion PLC, Alexander House, 85 Frampton St, London, NV8 8NQ, England.

Tel: +44 (0)990 134224

Fax: +44 (0)990 561046

Customer Services

Tel: +44 (0)990 143050

Fax: +44 (0)990 561046

Technical Support

Tel: +44 (0)990 143061

Dealers

Byson Computers. Tel +44 (0)1635 869480

Clove Technology, 43 Springbank Rd, Bournemouth, BH7 7EL.

Tel: +44 (0)1202 302796

Fax: +44 (0)1202 300419

Interdata Developments. Bridge program. Tel: +44 (0)161 7922871

Ipso Facto. Tel: +44 (0)115 9735482

Mobile software. London Restaurant and Hotel database Tel: +44 (0)181 906 0002.

Paradigm Technology, 71 Thames Park, Lester Way, Wallingford, Oxon, OX10 9TA.

Specialists in data collection and barcoding.

Tel: +44 (0)1491 822600

Fax: +44 (0)1491 822601

Pico Direct, The Technology Centre, Weston Farm, The Street, Albury, Surrey, GU5 9BZ. Specialists in mobile computer add-ons such as modem, cellular data cards and connection kits.

Tel: +44 (0)1483 202022

Rovoreed Ltd, New House Cottage, Cubblington, Madeley, Herefordshire, HR2 9NX.

Tel: +44 (0)1981 250026

Software Engineering. League Lexicon. Tel: +44 (0)1223 372458

Symantec. Publishers of the ACT! contact manager. Tel: +44 (0)1628 592320

Widget Software. Comprehensive catalogue of products including own software publishing.

Tel: +44 (0)1438 815444

Windmill Computing. Tel: +44 (0)161 7991878

Repair

POS. Pinnock Organiser Service are authorised to service the full range of Psion machines and accessories, with the exception of the 3Fax. For domestic customers they aim for a turnaround time of three days. Contact Paul Pinnock.

Tel: +44 (0)181 6779246 or 0831 194985 (mobile)

Contacts

Psion is represented in many countries around the globe and the details change from time to time. The best policy therefore is to call Psion at one of their main offices to ask for details of your local dealer. There are also listings of dealers on the Psion UK and US Internet sites:

http://www.psion.com

http://www.psioninc.com/

These are the main Psion office telephone numbers:

Psion UK Technical support 0990 143061, sales 0990 143050, fax 0990 561046, switchboard +44 (0)171 3174100

Psion US Sales hotline (free in US) 1-800 997 7466, +1 508 371 0310, fax: +1 508 371 9611, (west coast) +1 415 373 1234, fax +1 415 373 1233

Psion Germany +49 6172 6630, fax: +49 6172 663100

Psion Asia   +65 438 3200, fax: +65 438 3211

Appendix F

Programming

You can write your own programs for the Psion Series 3 and the programming language called OPL is built-in. Your Psion Series 3 is a mere handful of silicon and plastic without programs. Programs tell the components what to do. Your Psion Series 3 is a bit like a mechanical piano. You can play it directly from the keyboard (by choosing from a menu or typing instructions at a prompt) or you can play back a preprepared piece of music which comes on a roll of card with holes punched in it (running a program). Were these early computers I ask myself?

Your Psion Series 3 plays an altogether more sophisticated tune but the principle is the same. The basic unit of a program is a single instruction. A program is made up from building blocks known as routines, procedures and functions, each of which are made up of instructions. The instructions are carried out under the control of structures such as loops which repeat groups of instructions. Decision making commands send the program down particular paths depending on the state of the computer.

The programs don't grow on trees but are typed into the computer by a programmer into a text editor. Editors are important things for programmers. They are a special kind of wordprocessor designed to look after the layout of the program, to make it more understandable, to aid the productive entry of code through special key presses etc, and to check the program for errors, reporting them sensibly back to the programmer. The Psion Series 3 has its own built-in program editor.

Modern programming can also involve describing the program in diagrammatic or graphical terms, which are then converted automatically into code of a more conventional nature.High level – which means near English language – program instructions need to be converted to something the computer can understand. This is carried out by an interpreter or compiler.

A human interpreter at the European Parliament listens to what is being said in one language, for a few words, a few sentences at a time, and then passes the information on in a different language. This is also what a computer language interpreter does, in fact interpreting each command line at a time and passing on its interpretation to the computer's electronics.

A compiler is a bit more like a human language translator, though a bit quicker. It takes in the complete document (the program) and translates it all, making more than one pass over it if necessary, looking up bits in its dictionary (libraries) and, only when finished, sending the complete translation to the Psion Series 3's processor.

The main consequences for programmers are usually to do with the speed of the finished program. An interpreter is held up when running a program by having to go to and from the processor and program. A compiler takes longer to translate the program but only when it is compiling a new faster version of the program (compile time). When this faster version is run (run time) there is no hold up to speak of. This latter technique is the one which is used by the Psion OPL language.

OPL is the most popular programming language on the Psion Series 3 because it is built into every machine. OPL is similar to a very popular computer language called BASIC, a standard way of programming on many of the world's personal computers.

Oval Time

OPL is capable of producing top class applications but Psion have moved on to provide OVAL, a Visual Basic compatible programming environment. Visual Basic is the most popular way to program a desktop PC so many desktop programs can now be quickly converted for Psion and new programs being developed in Visual Basic can be developed for Psion in parallel. This should ensure that the best programs still end up on the Psion platform.

OVAL runs under Windows on a PC and features:

- visual layout of controls on forms.
- a code editor with syntax colour highlighting.
- a fully featured debugger.
- extensive on-line help.

- advanced resource file support.

- automatic downloading of applications and data files to the EPOC/16 platform.

The EPOC/32 platform from Psion supports a 32-bit version of OVAL.

So if you catch the Psion programming bug, there's plenty of scope. Psion Software, a new company set up to support the development of Psion applications, will be able to help any would-be Psion professional developers.

OPL Editor

Although the art of programming is beyond the scope of this book, it's worth taking a quick look at the OPL editor.

```
PROC TEST:                                    │Opl
 • LOCAL a%,a$(255)                           │◆No
 • DEFAULTWIN 1                               │ Ou
 • yxBORDER 1,1
 • REM This code
▶• dINIT "Produces this dialog"
 • • dTEXT "","and you can have:",2
 • • dCHOICE a%,"Choice lists:","This,That"
 • • dEDIT a$,"Edit boxes:",12
 • • dBUTTONS "Even",69,"Buttons",66
 • DIALOG
ENDP
```

The menus are familiar because many are shared with Word. The big difference is the Prog(ram) menu. Here you find the tools for getting a working program going. The Translate options convert the code you have typed into the editor into a program which the computer can understand. If the translation is successful you are prompted to run it. Show error helps you debug i.e. find errors in the program. Run sets an existing program going.

Hot-key Handy Reference

Hot-keys are a combination of Psion key (∪) and another key or a combination of Shift key (Shift), Psion key (∪) and another key. On Pocket Book II, the Acorn key takes the place of the Psion key.

System

Disk

Directory	∪*
Make directory	∪-
Remove directory	∪F
Name directory	∪H
Default directory	Shift∪H
Copy disk	Shift∪C

File

New file	∪N
Copy file	∪C
Delete file	∪D
Rename file	∪R
File attributes	∪T

Backup files	Shift∪B
Restore files	Shift∪R

Apps

Install	∪I
Install standard	∪J
Remove	∪/
Assign button	∪A
Exit application	Shift∪J
Exit all applications	Shift∪A
Kill applications	Shift∪K

Info

Set owner	∪P
Memory info	∪M
Disk info	∪K
Battery	∪B
Usage monitor	∪U
About Series 3	∪V
About application	Shift∪V

Control

Sound	∪S
Printer	∪Y
Auto switchoff	∪O
Dialling	Shift∪D
Evaluate formats	Shift∪E
Number formats	Shift∪F
Status window	Shift∪W

Special

Set preferences	∪Q
Password	∪W
Remote links	∪L
Create new list	∪E
Create new group	∪G
Zoom in	∪Z
Zoom out	Shift∪Z
Normal	Shift∪N
Memory	Shift∪M

Additional

File finder	highlight file and Tab
File finder file list	highlight file and Control Tab

File Finder

Tag	+
Untag	-
Tag all	*
Untag all	/

Data

File

New file	∪N
Open file	∪O
Save as	∪A
Merge in	∪M
Compress file	∪K

Edit

Insert text	∪I
Copy text	∪C
Bring text	∪B
Evaluate	∪E
Update entry	∪U
Delete entry	∪D
Edit labels	∪L

Search

Find previous	∪R
Find next	∪F
Start at current entry	∪G
Find by label	∪S
Jump to entry	∪J

Display

Set tabs	∪T
Wrap on	∪W
Hide labels	∪H

Special

Zoom in	∪Z
Zoom out	Shift∪Z

Print setup	∪Y	Jump to page	∪J
Print preview	∪*	Paginate	∪/
Print	∪P		
Exit	∪X	**Word**	
Find	Shift∪F	Expand outline	∪+
Change	Shift∪C	Collapse outline	∪-
Add	Shift∪A	Set outline level	∪H
Setup ◆ list	Shift∪◆	Use printer layout	∪L
		Password	∪W

Word

File

New file	∪N
Open file	∪O
Save as	∪A
Save as template	∪D
Save	∪S
Revert	∪V
Merge in	∪M

Edit

Insert text	∪I
Copy text	∪C
Bring text	∪B
Highlight all text	Shift∪L
Evaluate	∪E

Search

Find text	∪F
Find again	∪G
Replace	∪R
Count	∪K

Paragraphs

Font	Shift∪F
Indents	Shift∪I
Tabs	Shift∪T
Alignment	Shift∪A
Spacing	Shift∪S

Styles

Style gallery	Shift∪G
Style housekeeping	Shift∪H
Emphasis gallery	Shift∪E
Emphasis housekeeping	Shift∪K

Style housekeeping sub menu

Styles

Define	∪D
Apply	∪A
Rename	∪N
Delete	∪X
Find	∪F

Emphasis housekeeping

Emphases

Define	∪D

Apply	∪A	Bring	∪B
Rename	∪N	Change entry details	∪D
Delete	∪X	Change entry date	Shift∪M
Find	∪F	Change entry type	Shift∪C
		New entry	∪E

Special

Set preferences	∪O

Entry

Zoom in	∪Z	Set alarm for entry	∪L
Zoom out	Shift∪Z	Edit memo	∪+
Print setup	∪Y	Cross out entry	∪-
Print preview	∪*	Repeat entry	∪R
Print	∪P	Examine repeat	∪H
Exit, lose changes	Shift∪X	Set style for entry	∪S
Exit	∪X	Set year symbol for entry	∪/

◆

Normal	Shift∪N	**Search**	
Outline	Shift∪O	Find	∪F

Agenda

File		Find again	∪G
New file	∪N	Find next overlap	Shift∪O
Open file	∪O	Go to previous entry	Shift∪F
Save as	∪A	Go to next entry	Shift∪G
Merge in	∪M	Jump to date	∪J
Tidy/extract	∪T	Calendar	Shift∪J
Compress file	∪K	View all repeats	∪V

Edit

To-do-lists

Insert entry	∪I	New to-do-list	Shift∪N
Copy	∪C	Rename to-do-list	Shift∪R
		Delete to-do-list	Shift∪K
		Position to-do entry	Shift∪P

To-do list settings	⌣U

Special

Set preferences	⌣Q
Wrap off	⌣W
Zoom in	⌣Z
Zoom out	Shift⌣Z
Print setup	⌣Y
Print preview	⌣*
Print	⌣P
Exit	⌣X

◆

Day view	Shift⌣D
Week view	Shift⌣W
Year view	Shift⌣Y
To-do view	Shift⌣T
Anniversary view	Shift⌣A
List view	Shift⌣L
Examine repeat	⌣H
Set style for entry	⌣S
Set year symbol for entry	⌣/
Set up ◆ list	Shift⌣◆

View preferences sub menu

Day view	⌣D
Week view	⌣W
Year view	⌣Y
To-do view	⌣T
Anniversary view	⌣A
List view	⌣L

Entry preferences sub menu

Day entry defaults	⌣E
Anniversary defaults	⌣B
To-do entry defaults	⌣U
General preferences	⌣G

Time

Settings

Time and date	⌣T
Summer times	⌣S
Home city	⌣H
Start of week	⌣B
Workdays	⌣W
Formats	⌣F

Alarm

Set alarm	⌣A
Delete alarm	⌣D
Disable alarm	⌣-
View next alarms	⌣V

World

File

New file	⌣N
Open file	⌣O

Edit

Add city	⌣A
Update city	⌣U
Delete city	⌣D
Update country	⌣M
Current country only	⌣L

Special

Set home city	∪H
Distance units	∪K
Digital clocks	∪C
Exit	∪X

Sound Recorder

File

New file	∪N
Open file	∪O

Repeats

Set repeat	∪R
Adjust for alarm	∪A

Special

Set preferences	∪Q
Exit	∪X

Calc

Trig

sin(x)	∪S
cos(x)	∪C
tan(x)	∪T
asin(x)	Shift∪S
acos(x)	Shift∪C
atan(x)	Shift∪T

Powers

x^2	∪P
square root	∪Q
1/x	∪V

Logs

ln(x)	∪L
e^x	∪E
log(x)	∪G
10^x	∪H

Special

Format	∪F
Use radians	∪D
Load OPL	∪O
New list	∪N
Copy from list	∪K
Zoom in	∪Z
Zoom out	Shift∪Z
Exit	∪X

Other

Delete character to left of cursor
Delete

Delete character to right of cursor
Shift Delete

Move one screenful
∪up/down arrow
keys

Move top/bottom
Control∪up/down
arrow keys

Highlight next character
Shift left/right arrow keys

Highlight next line
Shift up/down arrow keys

Highlight current word
Control Shift∪ left arrow key

Highlight current paragraph
Control Shift∪right arrow key

Delete to the beginning of line
∪Delete

Delete to the end of line
Shift∪Delete

Move highlight to bottom of list
Tab

Specify filelist   Control Tab

Specify filelist   Control Enter

Open file without closing current file
Shift Enter

Display/Hide clock   Control Menu

Index

Find Your Way

The chapters in this book are arranged in a logical manner in that topic areas are introduced and discussed together. Therefore if you are not totally sure where to look for a particular item of information the chapter headings and sub-head details listed in the Contents pages at the start of this book are as good a place as any to look! This index contains pointers to major uses of the item under scrutiny. If you are looking for a particular aspect of an item, find it in the index and then look at this page and in the page or two following.

T

Free Disk Order Form

We've compiled a 'best of' disk of freeware and shareware for your Psion Series 3c, 3a or Siena. We've chosen a variety of programs, from utilities to games, which we think will give you a useful start with your new palmtop computer at a p&p price. The floppy disk is in PC 1.44 MSDOS format so you'll need a means of copying to your Psion i.e. PsiWin, Serial Link etc. All the programs run on all models.

Use this form or copy the details into a separate letter and send it to the address below. Or ring with your credit card.

Please rush me a copy of Total! Psion disk:

Total! Psion disk @ £3.00 postage and packing   £ ....

Total: £ ....

I enclose Cheque/Postal Order/Credit Card* for £   .   p.

Name ....

Address ....

....

Post Code ....

Contact phone number ....

Credit card number ....

Expiry date ....

Signed ....

E&OE. * delete those that do not apply.

Please send your cheques payable to *Bruce Smith Books Ltd* to:

**Bruce Smith Books Ltd, PO Box 382,
St. Albans, Herts, AL2 3JD**

Telephone credit card orders on: +44 (0)1604 832149